Making Dispute Resolution More Effective – MAP Peer Review Report, Isle of Man (Stage 2)

INCLUSIVE FRAMEWORK ON BEPS: ACTION 14

BETTER POLICIES FOR BETTER LIVES

This document, as well as any data and map included herein, are without prejudice to the status of or sovereignty over any territory, to the delimitation of international frontiers and boundaries and to the name of any territory, city or area.

Please cite this publication as:
OECD (2022), *Making Dispute Resolution More Effective – MAP Peer Review Report, Isle of Man (Stage 2): Inclusive Framework on BEPS: Action 14*, OECD/G20 Base Erosion and Profit Shifting Project, OECD Publishing, Paris, *https://doi.org/10.1787/fd56cc8d-en*.

ISBN 978-92-64-95626-1 (print)
ISBN 978-92-64-37826-1 (pdf)

OECD/G20 Base Erosion and Profit Shifting Project
ISSN 2313-2604 (print)
ISSN 2313-2612 (online)

Foreword

The integration of national economies and markets has increased substantially in recent years, putting a strain on the international tax rules, which were designed more than a century ago. Weaknesses in the current rules create opportunities for base erosion and profit shifting (BEPS), requiring bold moves by policy makers to restore confidence in the system and ensure that profits are taxed where economic activities take place and value is created.

Following the release of the report *Addressing Base Erosion and Profit Shifting* in February 2013, OECD and G20 countries adopted a 15-point Action Plan to address BEPS in September 2013. The Action Plan identified 15 actions along three key pillars: introducing coherence in the domestic rules that affect cross-border activities, reinforcing substance requirements in the existing international standards, and improving transparency as well as certainty.

After two years of work, measures in response to the 15 actions were delivered to G20 Leaders in Antalya in November 2015. All the different outputs, including those delivered in an interim form in 2014, were consolidated into a comprehensive package. The BEPS package of measures represents the first substantial renovation of the international tax rules in almost a century. Once the new measures become applicable, it is expected that profits will be reported where the economic activities that generate them are carried out and where value is created. BEPS planning strategies that rely on outdated rules or on poorly co-ordinated domestic measures will be rendered ineffective.

Implementation is now the focus of this work. The BEPS package is designed to be implemented via changes in domestic law and practices, and in tax treaties. With the negotiation of a multilateral instrument (MLI) having been finalised in 2016 to facilitate the implementation of the treaty related BEPS measures, over 90 jurisdictions are covered by the MLI. The entry into force of the MLI on 1 July 2018 paves the way for swift implementation of the treaty related measures. OECD and G20 countries also agreed to continue to work together to ensure a consistent and co-ordinated implementation of the BEPS recommendations and to make the project more inclusive. Globalisation requires that global solutions and a global dialogue be established which go beyond OECD and G20 countries.

A better understanding of how the BEPS recommendations are implemented in practice could reduce misunderstandings and disputes between governments. Greater focus on implementation and tax administration should therefore be mutually beneficial to governments and business. Proposed improvements to data and analysis will help support ongoing evaluation of the quantitative impact of BEPS, as well as evaluating the impact of the countermeasures developed under the BEPS Project.

As a result, the OECD established the OECD/G20 Inclusive Framework on BEPS (Inclusive Framework), bringing all interested and committed countries and jurisdictions on an equal footing in the Committee on Fiscal Affairs and all its subsidiary bodies. The

Inclusive Framework, which already has more than 135 members, is monitoring and peer reviewing the implementation of the minimum standards as well as completing the work on standard setting to address BEPS issues. In addition to BEPS members, other international organisations and regional tax bodies are involved in the work of the Inclusive Framework, which also consults business and the civil society on its different work streams.

This report was approved by the Inclusive Framework on 19 November 2021 and prepared for publication by the OECD Secretariat.

Table of contents

Figure

Abbreviations and acronyms

APA	Advance Pricing Arrangement
FTA	Forum on Tax Administration
MAP	Mutual Agreement Procedure
OECD	Organisation for Economic Co-operation and Development

Executive summary

The Isle of Man has a modest tax treaty network with almost 25 tax treaties. The Isle of Man further has very limited experience with resolving MAP cases. One other MAP case was initiated in 2018 and closed in 2019. Overall the Isle of Man meets almost all of the elements of the Action 14 Minimum Standard. Where it has deficiencies, the Isle of Man worked to address them, which has been monitored in stage 2 of the process. In this respect, the Isle of Man solved some of the identified deficiencies.

All of the Isle of Man's tax treaties contain a provision relating to MAP. Those treaties generally follow paragraphs 1 through 3 of Article 25 of the OECD Model Tax Convention. Its treaty network is largely consistent with the requirements of the Action 14 Minimum Standard, except mainly for the fact that:

- Approximately 12% of the Isle of Man's 24 tax treaties do not contain the equivalent of Article 25(1) of the OECD Model Tax Convention (OECD, 2017), whereby the majority of these treaties do not contain the equivalent of Article 25(1), first sentence, either as it read prior to the adoption of the Action 14 final report (OECD, 2015b) or as amended by that report and/or the timeline to file a MAP request is shorter than three years from the first notification of the action resulting in taxation not in accordance with the provision of the tax treaty.

- Approximately 12% of the Isle of Man's 24 tax treaties do not contain the equivalent of Article 25(2), first sentence, of the OECD Model Tax Convention (OECD, 2017) requiring its competent authority to endeavour to resolve the MAP case with the other competent authority.

In order to be fully compliant with all four key areas of an effective dispute resolution mechanism under the Action 14 Minimum Standard, the Isle of Man needs to update a certain number of its tax treaties. In this respect, the Isle of Man signed and ratified the Multilateral Instrument. Through this instrument some of its tax treaties have been modified to fulfil the requirements under the Action 14 Minimum Standard. Where treaties will not be modified, upon entry into force of this Multilateral Instrument for the treaties concerned, the Isle of Man reported that it intends to update all of its tax treaties via bilateral negotiations to be compliant with the requirements under the Action 14 Minimum Standard. For the four tax treaties that need a bilateral modification in order to be in line with such requirements, the Isle of Man reported that for one, negotiations were finalised, while negotiations are pending for another treaty. For the remaining two tax treaties, the Isle of Man is awaiting a response from the treaty partners to its request for the initiation of bilateral negotiations.

As the Isle of Man has no bilateral APA programme in place, there were no elements to assess regarding the prevention of disputes.

The Isle of Man in principle meets the requirements regarding the availability and access to MAP under the Action 14 Minimum Standard. It provides access to MAP in all eligible cases, although it has since 1 January 2016 not received any MAP request from taxpayers. Furthermore, the Isle of Man has in place a documented bilateral consultation or notification process for those situations in which its competent authority considers the objection raised by taxpayers in a MAP request as not justified. Finally, the Isle of Man has clear and comprehensive guidance on the availability of MAP and how it applies this procedure in practice.

Concerning the average time needed to close MAP cases, the MAP statistics for the Isle of Man for the period 2016-20 are as follows:

2016-20	Opening inventory 1/1/2016	Cases started	Cases closed	End Inventory 31/12/2020	Average time to close cases (in months)*
Attribution/allocation cases	0	0	0	0	N/A
Other cases	0	1	1	0	13.55
Total	0	1	1	0	13.55

*The average time taken for resolving MAP cases for post-2015 cases follows the MAP Statistics Reporting Framework. There were no pre-2016 cases pending on 1 January 2016.

As mentioned previously, during the 2016-20 period, the Isle of Man has only been involved in one "other" MAP case. The case concerned a post-2015 case and was closed within the pursued 24-month average.

Furthermore, the Isle of Man meets all the other requirements under the Action 14 Minimum Standard in relation to the resolution of MAP cases. The Isle of Man's competent authority operates fully independently from the audit function of the tax authorities and the performance indicators used are appropriate to perform the MAP function.

Lastly, the Isle of Man in principle meets the requirements under the Action 14 Minimum Standard as regards the implementation of MAP agreements. Since the Isle of Man did not enter into any MAP agreements that required implementation by the Isle of Man in 2016-20, no problems have surfaced regarding the implementation throughout the peer review process.

References

OECD (2015a), *Model Tax Convention on Income and on Capital 2014 (Full Version)*, OECD Publishing, Paris, https://dx.doi.org/10.1787/9789264239081-en.

OECD (2015b), "Making Dispute Resolution Mechanisms More Effective, Action 14 – 2015 Final Report", in *OECD/G20 Base Erosion and Profit Shifting Project*, OECD Publishing, Paris, https://dx.doi.org/10.1787/9789264241633-en.

OECD (2017), *Model Tax Convention on Income and on Capital 2017 (Full Version)*, OECD Publishing, Paris, https://dx.doi.org/10.1787/g2g972ee-en.

Introduction

Available mechanisms in the Isle of Man to resolve tax treaty-related disputes

The Isle of Man has entered into 24 tax treaties on income (and/or capital), 23 of which are in force.[1] These 24 treaties are being applied to an equal number of jurisdictions. All of these treaties provide for a mutual agreement procedure for resolving disputes on the interpretation and application of the provisions of the tax treaty. In addition, six of the 24 treaties provide for an arbitration procedure as a final stage to the mutual agreement procedure.[2]

Under the tax treaties the Isle of Man entered into, the competent authority function to conduct mutual agreement procedure ("**MAP**") is delegated to the Head of the Tax Administration. As the Isle of Man reported that it does receive very few MAP requests, it does not have a separate MAP team. In practice, MAP cases are being handled by a Deputy Assessor.

The Isle of Man issued guidance on the governance and administration of the mutual agreement procedure in the form of a guidance note, which was last updated in December 2020 and is available at:

https://www.gov.im/media/1364504/gn-57-map-guide-december-2020-update.pdf

Developments in the Isle of Man since 1 April 2019

Developments in relation to the tax treaty network

In the stage 1 peer review report of the Isle of Man, it is reflected that one of the Isle of Man's 24 tax treaties has not entered into force. This concerns the treaty with Belgium (2009). The Isle of Man has ratified this treaty, while Belgium has not yet, which has not changed since the adoption of the stage 1 report. Since 1 April 2019, the Isle of Man signed amending protocols to the treaties with Finland (2020) and Guernsey (2019). An amending protocol with Guernsey has entered into force while the other amending protocol with Finland has not. The amending protocols with Finland and Guernsey amend the MAP provision in those treaties allowing taxpayers to file a MAP request to the competent authorities of either contracting state.

Furthermore, on 7 June 2017 the Isle of Man signed the Multilateral Convention to Implement Tax Treaty Related Measures to Prevent Base Erosion and Profit Shifting ("**Multilateral Instrument**"), to adopt, where necessary, modifications to the MAP article under its tax treaties with a view to be compliant with the Action 14 Minimum Standard in respect of all the relevant tax treaties. The Isle of Man deposited its instrument of ratification of this instrument on 25 October 2017, following which the Multilateral Instrument for the Isle of Man entered into force on 1 July 2018.[3] With the deposition of the instrument of ratification, the Isle of Man also submitted its list of notifications and reservations to that instrument. In relation to the Action 14 Minimum Standard, the Isle of Man has not made any reservations to Article 16 of the Multilateral Instrument (concerning the mutual agreement procedure).

For those tax treaties that were in the stage 1 peer review report considered not to be in line with one or more elements of the Action 14 Minimum Standard and that will not be modified by the Multilateral Instrument, the Isle of Man reported that it strives updating them through future bilateral negotiations. In the stage 1 peer review report, it is stated that in 2018 and 2019 the Isle of Man sent out letters to the relevant treaty partners with the request on whether they wish to amend the treaties to meet the requirements under the Action 14 Minimum Standard, and agreed with one treaty partner on an amending protocol to the treaty. In total, four of the Isle of Man's tax treaties need a bilateral modification in order to be in line with the requirements under the Action 14 Minimum Standard. With respect to these four tax treaties, the Isle of Man reported that for one, negotiations were finalised, while negotiations are pending for another treaty. For the remaining two tax treaties, the Isle of Man is still awaiting a response from the treaty partners to its request for the initiation of bilateral negotiations to amend the treaties to meet the requirements under the Action 14 Minimum Standard.

Basis for the peer review process

Outline of the peer review process

The peer review process entails an evaluation of the Isle of Man's implementation of the Action 14 Minimum Standard through an analysis of its legal and administrative framework relating to the mutual agreement procedure, as governed by its tax treaties, domestic legislation and regulations, as well as its MAP programme guidance and the practical application of that framework. The review process performed is desk-based and conducted through specific questionnaires completed by the Isle of Man, its peers and taxpayers.

The process consists of two stages: a peer review process (stage 1) and a peer monitoring process (stage 2). In stage 1, the Isle of Man's implementation of the Action 14 Minimum Standard as outlined above is evaluated, which has been reflected in a peer review report that has been adopted by the BEPS Inclusive Framework on 14 August 2018. This report identifies the strengths and shortcomings of the Isle of Man in relation to the implementation of this standard and provides for recommendations on how these shortcomings should be addressed. The stage 1 report is published on the website of the OECD.[4] Stage 2 is launched within one year upon the adoption of the peer review report by the BEPS Inclusive Framework through an update report by the Isle of Man. In this update report, the Isle of Man reflected (i) what steps it has already taken, or are to be taken, to address any of the shortcomings identified in the peer review report and (ii) any plans or changes to its legislative and/or administrative framework concerning the implementation of the Action 14 Minimum Standard. The update report forms the basis for the completion of the peer review process, which is reflected in this update to the stage 1 peer review report.

Outline of the treaty analysis

For the purpose of this report and the statistics below, in assessing whether the Isle of Man is compliant with the elements of the Action 14 Minimum Standard that relate to a specific treaty provision, the newly negotiated treaties or the treaties as modified by a protocol, as described above, were taken into account, even if it concerned a modification or a replacement of an existing treaty. Furthermore, the 24 tax treaties the Isle of Man has entered into include treaties with Denmark, the Faroe Islands, Finland, Iceland, Greenland, Norway and Sweden. With these seven jurisdictions, the Isle of Man has entered into separate treaties that have a limited scope of application, one of which relates to transfer pricing and one to certain categories of income of individuals. In this situation, the number of such treaties is regarded as one for the purpose of this peer review report. Reference is made to Annex A for the overview of the Isle of Man's tax treaties regarding the mutual agreement procedure.

Timing of the process and input received by peers and taxpayers

Stage 1 of the peer review process was for the Isle of Man launched on 27 March 2019, with the sending of questionnaires to the Isle of Man and its peers. The FTA MAP Forum has approved the stage 1 peer review report of the Isle of Man in September 2019, with the subsequent approval by the BEPS Inclusive Framework on 11 December 2019. On 11 December 2020, the Isle of Man submitted its update report, which initiated stage 2 of the process.

The period for evaluating the Isle of Man's implementation of the Action 14 Minimum Standard ranges from 1 January 2016 to 31 March 2019 and formed the basis for the stage 1 peer review report. The period of review for stage 2 started on 1 April 2019 and depicts all developments as from that date until 31 December 2020.

One peer, Australia, provided input during stage 1. This peer did not have MAP cases with the Isle of Man that started in 2016, 2017 or 2018. Its input only related to the treaty provisions, not to experiences in handling and resolving MAP cases. During stage 2, the United Kingdom provided input. For this stage, this peer represents approximately 100% of post-2015 MAP cases in the Isle of Man's inventory that started in 2016-20. This peer provided information that it has reached a new competent authority agreement with the Isle of Man on company residence tie-breaker, which was done very easily and quickly.

Input by the Isle of Man and co-operation throughout the process

During stage 1, The Isle of Man provided extensive answers in its questionnaire, which was submitted on time. The Isle of Man was very responsive in the course of the drafting of the peer review report by responding timely and comprehensively to requests for additional information, and provided further clarity where necessary. In addition, the Isle of Man provided the following information:

- MAP profile[5]
- MAP statistics[6] according to the MAP Statistics Reporting Framework (see below).

Concerning stage 2 of the process, the Isle of Man submitted its update report on time and the information included therein was extensive. The Isle of Man was co-operative during stage 2 and the finalisation of the peer review process.

Finally, the Isle of Man is a member of the FTA MAP Forum and has shown good co-operation during the peer review process.

Overview of MAP caseload in the Isle of Man

The analysis of the Isle of Man's MAP caseload for stage 1 relates to the period starting on 1 January 2016 and ending on 31 December 2018. For stage 2 the period ranges from 1 January 2019 to 31 December 2020. Both periods are taken into account in this report for analysing the MAP statistics of the Isle of Man. The analysis of the Isle of Man's MAP caseload therefore relates to the period starting on 1 January 2016 and ending 31 December 2020 ("**Statistics Reporting Period**"). According to the statistics provided by the Isle of Man, its MAP caseload during this period was as follows:

2016-20	Opening inventory 1/1/2016	Cases started	Cases Closed	End Inventory 31/12/2020
Attribution/allocation cases	0	0	0	0
Other cases	0	1	1	0
Total	0	1	1	0

General outline of the peer review report

This report includes an evaluation of the Isle of Man's implementation of the Action 14 Minimum Standard. The report comprises the following four sections:

A. Preventing disputes

B. Availability and access to MAP

C. Resolution of MAP cases

D. Implementation of MAP agreements.

Each of these sections is divided into elements of the Action 14 Minimum Standard, as described in the terms of reference to monitor and review the implementing of the BEPS Action 14 Minimum Standard to make dispute resolution mechanisms more effective ("**Terms of Reference**").[7] Apart from analysing the Isle of Man's legal framework and its administrative practice, the report also incorporates peer input. Furthermore, the report depicts the changes adopted and plans shared by the Isle of Man to implement elements of the Action 14 Minimum Standard where relevant. The conclusion of each element identifies areas for improvement (if any) and provides for recommendations how the specific area for improvement should be addressed.

The basis of this report is the outcome of the stage 1 peer review process, which has identified in each element areas for improvement (if any) and provides for recommendations how the specific area for improvement should be addressed. Following the outcome of the peer monitoring process of stage 2, each of the elements has been updated with a recent development section to reflect any actions taken or changes made on how recommendations have been addressed, or to reflect other changes in the legal and administrative framework of the Isle of Man relating to the implementation of the Action 14 Minimum Standard. Where it concerns changes to MAP guidance or statistics, these changes are reflected in the analysis sections of the elements, with a general description of the changes in the recent development sections.

The objective of the Action 14 Minimum Standard is to make dispute resolution mechanisms more effective and concerns a continuous effort. Where recommendations have been fully implemented, this has been reflected and the conclusion section of the relevant element has been modified accordingly, but the Isle of Man should continue to act in accordance with a given element of the Action 14 Minimum Standard, even if there is no area for improvement and recommendation for this specific element.

Notes

1. The tax treaties the Isle of Man has entered into are available at: https://www.gov.im/categories/tax-vat-and-your-money/income-tax-and-national-insurance/international-agreements/double-taxation-agreements/. The treaty that is signed but has not yet entered into force is with Belgium, although the Isle of Man already ratified this treaty. This newly negotiated treaty is taken into account in the treaty analysis. Reference is made to Annex A for the overview of the Isle of Man's tax treaties concerning the mutual agreement procedure.

   Furthermore, the 24 tax treaties the Isle of Man has entered into include treaties with Denmark, the Faroe Islands, Finland, Iceland, Greenland, Norway and Sweden. With these seven jurisdictions, the Isle of Man has entered into separate treaties that have a limited scope of application, one of which relates to transfer pricing and one to certain categories of income of individuals. In this situation, the number of such treaties is regarded as one for the purpose of this peer review report.

2. This concerns the treaties with Bahrain, Belgium, Guernsey, Jersey, Luxembourg and the United Kingdom.

3. Available at: www.oecd.org/tax/treaties/beps-mli-position-isle-of-man-instrument-deposit.pdf.

4. Available at: https://www.oecd.org/tax/beps/making-dispute-resolution-more-effective-map-peer-review-report-isle-of-man-stage-1-26d15793-en.htm.

5. Available at www.oecd.org/tax/dispute/Isle-of-Man-Dispute-Resolution-Profile.pdf.

6. The MAP statistics of the Isle of Man are included in Annex B and C of this report.

7. Terms of reference to monitor and review the implementing of the BEPS Action 14 Minimum Standard to make dispute resolution mechanisms more effective. Available at: www.oecd.org/tax/beps/beps-action-14-on-more-effective-dispute-resolution-peer-review-documents.pdf.

Part A

Preventing disputes

[A.1] Include Article 25(3), first sentence, of the OECD Model Tax Convention in tax treaties

> Jurisdictions should ensure that their tax treaties contain a provision which requires the competent authority of their jurisdiction to endeavour to resolve by mutual agreement any difficulties or doubts arising as to the interpretation or application of their tax treaties.

1.   Cases may arise concerning the interpretation or the application of tax treaties that do not necessarily relate to individual cases, but are more of a general nature. Inclusion of the first sentence of Article 25(3) of the OECD Model Tax Convention (OECD, 2017a) in tax treaties invites and authorises competent authorities to solve these cases, which may avoid submission of MAP requests and/or future disputes from arising, and which may reinforce the consistent bilateral application of tax treaties.

Current situation of the Isle of Man's tax treaties

2.   Out of the Isle of Man's 24 tax treaties, 21 contain a provision that is equivalent to Article 25(3), first sentence, of the OECD Model Tax Convention (OECD, 2017a) requiring their competent authority to endeavour to resolve by mutual agreement any difficulties or doubts arising as to the interpretation or application of the tax treaty. For two of the remaining three treaties, the scope of the provision is limited to difficulties or doubts arising as to the application of the treaty and the term "interpretation" is missing, following which they are considered as not being equivalent to the first sentence. The remaining treaty does not contain a provision at all that is based on the first sentence of Article 25(3), which, however, can be clarified by the fact that this treaty only includes one provision that falls in the scope of MAP. In other words, for this treaty there would not be any difficulties or doubts arising as to the interpretation or application of the tax treaty, other than that can already be dealt with in MAP. This treaty, therefore is considered to be in line with element A.1.

3.   The Isle of Man reported that where a tax treaty does not contain the full equivalent of Article 25(3), first sentence, of the OECD Model Tax Convention (OECD, 2017a), there are under its domestic legislation and/or administrative practice no obstructions that would prevent its competent authority to enter into discussions on the interpretation or application of the treaty.

4.   One peer provided input during stage 1 and mentioned that its treaty with the Isle of Man is a treaty with a limited scope that applies to a narrower range of circumstances than the MAP articles contained in comprehensive tax treaties. The peer further reported

that it has not sought to amend its MAP article in order to meet the requirements under the Action 14 minimum standard. It also did not indicate it was contacted by the Isle of Man for this purpose.

Recent developments

Bilateral modifications

5.   There are no recent developments as to new treaties or amendments to existing treaties being signed in relation to element A.1.

Multilateral Instrument

6.   The Isle of Man signed the Multilateral Instrument and deposited its instrument of ratification on 25 October 2017. The Multilateral Instrument for the Isle of Man entered into force on 1 July 2018.

7.   Article 16(4)(c)(i) of that instrument stipulates that Article 16(3), first sentence – containing the equivalent of Article 25(3), first sentence, of the OECD Model Tax Convention (OECD, 2017a) – will apply in the absence of a provision in tax treaties that is equivalent to Article 25(3), first sentence, of the OECD Model Tax Convention (OECD, 2017a). In other words, in the absence of this equivalent, Article 16(4)(c)(i) of the Multilateral Instrument will modify the applicable tax treaty to include such equivalent. However, this shall only apply if both contracting parties to the applicable tax treaty have listed this treaty as a covered tax agreement under the Multilateral Instrument and insofar as both notified, pursuant to Article 16(6)(d)(i), the depositary that this treaty does not contain the equivalent of Article 25(3), first sentence, of the OECD Model Tax Convention (OECD, 2017a).

8.   In regard of the two tax treaties identified above that are considered not to contain the equivalent of Article 25(3), first sentence, of the OECD Model Tax Convention (OECD, 2017a), the Isle of Man listed none of them as a covered tax agreement under the Multilateral Instrument. Therefore, at this stage, these two tax treaties will not be modified by the Multilateral Instrument to include the equivalent of Article 25(3), first sentence, of the OECD Model Tax Convention (OECD, 2017a).

Peer input

9.   The peer that provided input during stage 2 did not provide input in relation to their tax treaty with the Isle of Man.

Anticipated modifications

10.   The Isle of Man reported that for the two tax treaties that do not contain the equivalent of Article 25(3), first sentence, of the OECD Model Tax Convention (OECD, 2017a) will not be modified by the Multilateral Instrument, it is awaiting a response from the treaty partners to its request for the initiation of bilateral negotiations to amend the treaties to meet the requirements under the Action 14 Minimum Standard.

11.   The Isle of Man reported it will seek to include Article 25(3), first sentence, of the OECD Model Tax Convention (OECD, 2017a) in all of its future tax treaties.

Conclusion

	Areas for improvement	Recommendations
[A.1]	Two out of 23 tax treaties do not contain a provision that is equivalent to Article 25(3), first sentence, of the OECD Model Tax Convention (OECD, 2017a). These two treaties will not be modified by the Multilateral Instrument to include the required provision, but the Isle of Man has reached out to its treaty partners to request the initiation of bilateral negotiations, for which it is awaiting a response.	For the two treaties that do not contain the equivalent of Article 25(3), first sentence, of the OECD Model Tax Convention (OECD, 2017a) and that will not be modified by the Multilateral Instrument, the Isle of Man should, upon receipt of a response from the relevant treaty partners agreeing to include the required provision, work towards updating the treaties to include this provision

[A.2] Provide roll-back of bilateral APAs in appropriate cases

Jurisdictions with bilateral advance pricing arrangement ("APA") programmes should provide for the roll-back of APAs in appropriate cases, subject to the applicable time limits (such as statutes of limitation for assessment) where the relevant facts and circumstances in the earlier tax years are the same and subject to the verification of these facts and circumstances on audit.

12.   An APA is an arrangement that determines, in advance of controlled transactions, an appropriate set of criteria (e.g. method, comparables and appropriate adjustment thereto, critical assumptions as to future events) for the determination of the transfer pricing for those transactions over a fixed period of time.[1] The methodology to be applied prospectively under a bilateral or multilateral APA may be relevant in determining the treatment of comparable controlled transactions in previous filed years. The "roll-back" of an APA to these previous filed years may be helpful to prevent or resolve potential transfer pricing disputes.

The Isle of Man's APA programme

13.   The Isle of Man reported it does not have an APA programme in place, by which there is no possibility for providing roll-back of bilateral APAs to previous years.

Recent developments

14.   There are no recent developments with respect to element A.2.

Practical application of roll-back of bilateral APAs

15.   Peers provided no specific input in relation to element A.2 during stage 1 (1 January 2016-31 March 2019) and stage 2 (1 April 2019-31 December 2020).

Anticipated modifications

16.   The Isle of Man did not indicate that it anticipates any modifications in relation to element A.2.

Conclusion

	Areas for improvement	Recommendations
[A.2]	-	-

Note

1. This description of an APA based on the definition of an APA in the OECD Transfer Pricing Guidelines for Multinational Enterprises and Tax Administrations (OECD, 2017b).

References

OECD (2017a), *Model Tax Convention on Income and on Capital 2017 (Full Version)*, OECD Publishing, Paris, https://dx.doi.org/10.1787/g2g972ee-en.

OECD (2017b), *OECD Transfer Pricing Guidelines for Multinational Enterprises and Tax Administrations 2017*, https://dx.doi.org/10.1787/tpg-2017-en.

Part B

Availability and access to MAP

[B.1] Include Article 25(1) of the OECD Model Tax Convention in tax treaties

> Jurisdictions should ensure that their tax treaties contain a MAP provision which provides that when the taxpayer considers that the actions of one or both of the Contracting Parties result or will result for the taxpayer in taxation not in accordance with the provisions of the tax treaty, the taxpayer, may irrespective of the remedies provided by the domestic law of those Contracting Parties, make a request for MAP assistance, and that the taxpayer can present the request within a period of no less than three years from the first notification of the action resulting in taxation not in accordance with the provisions of the tax treaty.

17.   For resolving cases of taxation not in accordance with the provisions of the tax treaty, it is necessary that tax treaties include a provision allowing taxpayers to request a mutual agreement procedure and that this procedure can be requested irrespective of the remedies provided by the domestic law of the treaty partners. In addition, to provide certainty to taxpayers and competent authorities on the availability of the mutual agreement procedure, a minimum period of three years for submission of a MAP request, beginning on the date of the first notification of the action resulting in taxation not in accordance with the provisions of the tax treaty, is the baseline.

Current situation of the Isle of Man's tax treaties

Inclusion of Article 25(1), first sentence of the OECD Model Tax Convention

18.   Out of the Isle of Man's 24 tax treaties, three contain a provision equivalent to Article 25(1), first sentence, of the OECD Model Tax Convention (OECD, 2017), as amended by the Action 14 final report (OECD, 2015b) and allowing taxpayers to submit a MAP request to the competent authority of either state when they consider that the actions of one or both of the treaty partners result or will result for the taxpayer in taxation not in accordance with the provisions of the tax treaty and that can be requested irrespective of the remedies provided by domestic law of either state. Furthermore, ten treaties contain a provision equivalent to Article 25(1), first sentence, of the OECD Model Tax Convention (OECD, 2015a) as it read prior to the adoption of the Action 14 final report (OECD, 2015b), allowing taxpayers to submit a MAP request to the competent authority of the state in which they are resident.

19.   The remaining 11 treaties can be categorised as follows:

Provision	Number of tax treaties
A variation of Article 25(1), first sentence, of the OECD Model Tax Convention (OECD, 2015a) as it read prior to the adoption of the Action 14 final report (OECD, 2015b), whereby taxpayers can only submit a MAP request for transfer pricing adjustments, whereas the scope of the treaty also covers certain items of income concerning individuals.	2
A variation of Article 25(1), first sentence, of the OECD Model Tax Convention (OECD, 2015a) as it read prior to the adoption of the Action 14 final report (OECD, 2015b), whereby taxpayers can only submit a MAP request to the competent authority of the contracting state of which they are resident.	9

20.   The two treaties in the first row of the table are considered not to have the full equivalent of Article 25(1), first sentence, of the OECD Model Tax Convention (OECD, 2015a) as it read prior to the adoption of the Action 14 final report (OECD, 2015b), since the scope of the MAP provision is limited to one type of disputes, whereas the treaty has a broader scope of application. These treaties are therefore not in line with this part of element B.1.

21.   The nine treaties in the second row are also considered not to have the full equivalent of Article 25(1), first sentence, of the OECD Model Tax Convention (OECD, 2015a) as it read prior to the adoption of the Action 14 final report (OECD, 2015b), since taxpayers are not allowed to submit a MAP request in the state of which they are a national where the case comes under the non-discrimination article. However, eight out of these nine treaties are considered to be in line with this part of element B.1, since they do not contain a non-discrimination provision.

22.   For the remaining treaty, the non-discrimination provision is almost identical to Article 24(1) of the OECD Model Tax Convention (OECD, 2017) and applies both to nationals that are and are not resident of one of the contracting states. The omission of the full text of Article 25(1), first sentence, of the OECD Model Tax Convention (OECD, 2017) is therefore not clarified by the absence of or a limited scope of the non-discrimination provision, following which this treaty is not in line with this part of element B.1.

Inclusion of Article 25(1), second sentence of the OECD Model Tax Convention

23.   Out of the Isle of Man's 24 tax treaties, 21 contain a provision equivalent to Article 25(1), second sentence, of the OECD Model Tax Convention (OECD, 2017) allowing taxpayers to submit a MAP request within a period of no less than three years from the first notification of the action resulting in taxation not in accordance with the provisions of the particular tax treaty.

24.   For the remaining three treaties, the following analysis can be made:

Provision	Number of tax treaties
Filing period less than three years for a MAP request (two years)	1
Filing period of three years, but only relating to transfer pricing adjustments, while the scope of the treaty is broader in application	2

Peer input

25.   One peer provided input during stage 1 and mentioned that its treaty with the Isle of Man is a treaty with a limited scope that applies to a narrower range of circumstances than the MAP articles contained in comprehensive tax treaties. The peer further reported

that it has not sought to amend its MAP article in order to meet the requirements under the Action 14 minimum standard. It also did not confirm it was contacted by the Isle of Man for this purpose. In a response, the Isle of Man mentioned it has contacted the relevant treaty partner, as indicated above.

Practical application

Article 25(1), first sentence, of the OECD Model Tax Convention

26.　All of the Isle of Man's tax treaties that contain a MAP provision stipulate that taxpayers can submit a MAP request irrespective of domestic remedies. In this respect, the Isle of Man reported that tax treaties have effect as part of the Isle of Man's domestic law, such pursuant to section 104B(1) of the Income Tax Act of 1970. Section 104E(1) further defines that such effect exists despite any enactment or other document or other rule of law. As a consequence, the MAP process can be operated and a MAP agreement can be implemented irrespective of whether taxpayers have initiated domestic remedies for the same case under review or whether such remedies have been concluded. Up to date, the Isle of Man has not received any MAP requests for cases for which domestic remedies have been initiated or concluded.

Recent developments

Bilateral modifications

27.　The Isle of Man signed two amending protocols to existing treaties. The two amending protocols contain a provision that is equivalent to Article 25(1), first sentence, of the OECD Model Tax Convention (OECD, 2017) as amended by the Action 14 final report (OECD, 2015b) and allowing taxpayers to file a MAP request to either competent authority. One amending protocol has entered into force, while the other has not. The effects of the two amending protocols have been reflected in the analysis above where they have relevance.

Multilateral Instrument

28.　The Isle of Man signed the Multilateral Instrument and deposited its instrument of ratification on 25 October 2017. The Multilateral Instrument for the Isle of Man entered into force one 1 July 2018.

Article 25(1), first sentence of the OECD Model Tax Convention

29.　Article 16(4)(a)(i) of that instrument stipulates that Article 16(1), first sentence – containing the equivalent of Article 25(1), first sentence, of the OECD Model Tax Convention (OECD, 2017) as amended by the Action 14 final report (OECD, 2015b) and allowing the submission of MAP requests to the competent authority of either contracting state – will apply in place of or in the absence of a provision in tax treaties that is equivalent to Article 25(1), first sentence, of the OECD Model Tax Convention (OECD, 2015a) as it read prior to the adoption of the Action 14 final report (OECD, 2015b). However, this shall only apply if both contracting parties to the applicable tax treaty have listed this tax treaty as a covered tax agreement under the Multilateral Instrument and insofar as both notified the depositary, pursuant to Article 16(6)(a), that this treaty contains the equivalent of Article 25(1), first sentence, of the OECD Model Tax Convention (OECD, 2015a) as it read prior to the adoption of the Action 14 final report (OECD, 2015b). Article 16(4)(a)(i) will for a tax treaty not take effect if one of the treaty partners has, pursuant to Article 16(5)(a), reserved the right not to apply the first sentence of Article 16(1) of that instrument to all of its covered tax agreements.

30.   With the ratification of the Multilateral Instrument, the Isle of Man opted, pursuant to Article 16(4)(a)(i) of that instrument, to introduce in all of its tax treaties a provision that is equivalent to Article 25(1), first sentence, of the OECD Model Tax Convention (OECD, 2017) as amended by the Action 14 final report (OECD, 2015b), allowing taxpayers to submit a MAP request to the competent authority of either contracting state. In other words, where under the Isle of Man's tax treaties taxpayers currently have to submit a MAP request to the competent authority of the contracting state of which he is a resident, the Isle of Man opted to modify these treaties allowing taxpayers to submit a MAP request to the competent authority of either contracting state. In this respect, the Isle of Man listed eight of its 23 treaties as a covered tax agreement under the Multilateral Instrument and made, on the basis of Article 16(6)(a), for all of them the notification that they contain a provision that is equivalent to Article 25(1), first sentence, of the OECD Model Tax Convention (OECD, 2015a) as it read prior to the adoption of the Action 14 final report (OECD, 2015b).

31.   One of the eight relevant treaty partners reserved, pursuant to Article 16(5)(a), the right not to apply the first sentence of Article 16(1) to its existing tax treaties, with a view to allow taxpayers to submit a MAP request to the competent authority of either contracting state. Of the remaining seven treaty partners, six listed their treaty with the Isle of Man as having a provision that is equivalent of Article 25(1), first sentence, of the OECD Model Tax Convention (OECD, 2015a) as it read prior to the adoption of the Action 14 final report (OECD, 2015b).

32.   With respect to these six treaties, five treaty partners already deposited their instrument of ratification of the Multilateral Instrument, following which the Multilateral Instrument has entered into force for the treaties between the Isle of Man and these treaty partners, and therefore has modified these treaties to include the equivalent of Article 25(1), first sentence, of the OECD Model Tax Convention (OECD, 2017) as amended by the Action 14 final report (OECD, 2015b). For the remaining treaty, the instrument will, upon entry into force for the treaty, modify it to include this equivalent.

33.   Furthermore, for the seventh treaty, where the treaty partner did not make a notification on the basis of Article 16(6)(a), this treaty will be superseded by the Multilateral Instrument to include the equivalent of Article 25(1), first sentence, of the OECD Model Tax Convention (OECD, 2017) as amended by the Action 14 final report (OECD, 2015b).

34.   In view of the above and in relation to the three treaties identified in paragraphs 19-22 that are considered not to contain the equivalent of Article 25(1), first sentence, of the OECD Model Tax Convention (OECD, 2015a) as it read prior to the adoption of the final Action 14 final report (OECD, 2015b), the Isle of Man listed none of them as a covered tax agreement. Therefore, these three treaties will not be modified by the Multilateral Instrument.

Article 25(1), second sentence of the OECD Model Tax Convention

35.   With respect to the period of filing of a MAP request, Article 16(4)(a)(ii) of the Multilateral Instrument stipulates that Article 16(1), second sentence – containing the equivalent of Article 25(1), second sentence, of the OECD Model Tax Convention (OECD, 2017) – will apply where such period is shorter than three years from the first notification of the action resulting in taxation not in accordance with the provisions of a tax treaty. However, this shall only apply if both contracting parties to the applicable tax treaty have listed this treaty as a covered tax agreement under the Multilateral Instrument and insofar as

both notified, pursuant to Article 16(6)(b)(i), the depositary that this treaty does not contain the equivalent of Article 25(1), second sentence, of the OECD Model Tax Convention (OECD, 2017).

36.   In regard of the three tax treaties identified in paragraph 24 that contain a filing period for MAP requests of less than three years or that contain a filing period only concerning transfer pricing adjustments, the Isle of Man listed only one treaty as a covered tax agreement under the Multilateral Instrument and made for this treaty, pursuant to Article 16(6)(b)(i), a notification that it does not contain a provision described in Article 16(4)(a)(ii). The relevant treaty partner, being a signatory to the Multilateral Instrument, listed the treaty with the Isle of Man as a covered tax agreement under that instrument, and also made a notification pursuant to Article 16(6)(b)(i). With respect to this treaty, the relevant treaty partner has already deposited its instrument of ratification of the Multilateral Instrument, following which the Multilateral Instrument has entered into force for the treaty between the Isle of Man and this treaty partner, and therefore has modified this treaty to include the equivalent of Article 25(1), second sentence, of the OECD Model Tax Convention (OECD, 2017).

Peer input

37.   The peer that provided input during stage 2 did not provide input in relation to their tax treaty with the Isle of Man.

Anticipated modifications

38.   The Isle of Man reported that for the three tax treaties that do not contain the equivalent of Article 25(1), first and/or sentence, of the OECD Model Tax Convention (OECD, 2017), as it read prior to the adoption of the Action 14 final report (OECD, 2015b), and that will not be modified by the Multilateral Instrument, from two of the three treaty partners it is awaiting a response to its request for the initiation of bilateral negotiations to amend the treaties to meet the requirements under the Action 14 Minimum Standard, while negotiations are pending with the remaining treaty partner.

39.   The Isle of Man reported it will seek to include Article 25(1) of the OECD Model Tax Convention (OECD, 2017), as it read after the adoption of the Action 14 final report (OECD, 2015b), in all of its future tax treaties.

Conclusion

	Areas for improvement	Recommendations
[B.1]	One out of 24 tax treaties does not contain a provision that is equivalent to Article 25(1), first sentence, of the OECD Model Tax Convention (OECD, 2017). This tax treaty will not be modified by the Multilateral Instrument to include the required provision. With respect to this treaty, negotiations are pending.	For the treaty that does not contain the equivalent of Article 25(1), first sentence, of the OECD Model Tax Convention (OECD, 2017) and will not be modified by the Multilateral Instrument to include such equivalent, the Isle of Man should continue negotiations to include the required provision.
		This concerns a provision that is equivalent to Article 25(1), first sentence, of the OECD Model Tax Convention (OECD, 2017) either: a. as amended by the Action 14 final report (OECD, 2015b); or b. as it read prior to the adoption of the Action 14 final report (OECD, 2015b), thereby including the full sentence of such provision.

	Areas for improvement	Recommendations
[B.1]	Two out of 24 tax treaties do not contain a provision that is equivalent to Article 25(1), first sentence, of the OECD Model Tax Convention (OECD, 2017) and the timeline to file a MAP request is three years, but only applies to transfer pricing adjustments. None of these two tax treaties will be modified by the Multilateral Instrument to include the first and second sentence of Article 25(1). With respect to these treaties, the Isle of Man has reached out to its treaty partners to request the initiation of bilateral negotiations, for which it is awaiting a response.	As the two treaties that do not contain the equivalent of Article 25(1), first and second sentence, of the OECD Model Tax Convention (OECD, 2017) will not be modified by the Multilateral Instrument to include such equivalent, the Isle of Man should, upon receipt of a response from the relevant treaty partners agreeing to include the required provision, work towards updating the treaties to include this provision.

[B.2] Allow submission of MAP requests to the competent authority of either treaty partner, or, alternatively, introduce a bilateral consultation or notification process

> Jurisdictions should ensure that either (i) their tax treaties contain a provision which provides that the taxpayer can make a request for MAP assistance to the competent authority of either Contracting Party, or (ii) where the treaty does not permit a MAP request to be made to either Contracting Party and the competent authority who received the MAP request from the taxpayer does not consider the taxpayer's objection to be justified, the competent authority should implement a bilateral consultation or notification process which allows the other competent authority to provide its views on the case (such consultation shall not be interpreted as consultation as to how to resolve the case).

40.   In order to ensure that all competent authorities concerned are aware of MAP requests submitted, for a proper consideration of the request by them and to ensure that taxpayers have effective access to MAP in eligible cases, it is essential that all tax treaties contain a provision that either allows taxpayers to submit a MAP request to the competent authority:

i.   of either treaty partner; or, in the absence of such provision,

ii. where it is a resident, or to the competent authority of the state of which they are a national if their cases come under the non-discrimination article. In such cases, jurisdictions should have in place a bilateral consultation or notification process where a competent authority considers the objection raised by the taxpayer in a MAP request as being not justified.

Domestic bilateral consultation or notification process in place

41.   As discussed under element B.1, out of the Isle of Man's 24 treaties, three currently contain a provision equivalent to Article 25(1), first sentence, of the OECD Model Tax Convention (OECD, 2017) as amended by the Action 14 final report (OECD, 2015b), allowing taxpayers to submit a MAP request to the competent authority of either treaty partner. As was also discussed under element B.1, five of the remaining 21 treaties have been modified by the Multilateral Instrument to include such equivalent, and another two will, upon entry into force, be modified or superseded by the Multilateral Instrument to allow taxpayers to submit a MAP request to the competent authority of either treaty partner.

42.   The Isle of Man reported that it has introduced a documented bilateral consultation or notification process for those situations where its competent authority would consider the objection raised in a MAP request as not being justified.

Recent developments

43.   The Isle of Man reported that it has introduced a documented bilateral consultation or notification process for those situations where its competent authority would consider the objection raised in a MAP request as not being justified.

Practical application

Period 1 January 2016-31 March 2019 (stage 1)

44.   The Isle of Man reported that since 1 January 2016-31 March 2019 its competent authority has for none of the MAP requests it received decided that the objection raised by taxpayers in such request was not justified, which can be clarified that no such requests were received since that date. The 2016-18 MAP statistics submitted by the Isle of Man also show that none of its MAP cases were closed with the outcome "objection not justified".

45.   Peers did not provide input in relation to the Isle of Man's implementation of the Action 14 Minimum Standard.

Period 1 April 2019-31 December 2020 (stage 2)

46.   The Isle of Man reported that also since 1 April 2019 its competent authority has for none of the MAP requests it received decided that the objection raised by the taxpayer in its request was not justified. The 2019 and 2020 MAP statistics submitted by the Isle of Man confirm that none of its MAP cases were closed with the outcome "objection not justified".

47.   The peer that provided input during stage 2 did not provide input in relation to element B.2.

Anticipated modifications

48.   The Isle of Man did not indicate that it anticipates any modifications in relation to element B.2.

Conclusion

	Areas for improvement	Recommendations
[B.2]	-	-

[B.3] Provide access to MAP in transfer pricing cases

> Jurisdictions should provide access to MAP in transfer pricing cases.

49.   Where two or more tax administrations take different positions on what constitutes arm's length conditions for specific transactions between associated enterprises, economic double taxation may occur. Not granting access to MAP with respect to a treaty partner's transfer pricing adjustment, with a view to eliminating the economic double taxation that may arise from such adjustment, will likely frustrate the main objective of tax treaties. Jurisdictions should thus provide access to MAP in transfer pricing cases.

Legal and administrative framework

50.   Out of the Isle of Man's 24 tax treaties, 16 contain a provision equivalent to Article 9(2) of the OECD Model Tax Convention (OECD, 2017) requiring their state to make a correlative adjustment in case a transfer pricing adjustment is imposed by the treaty partner.[1]

51.   Of the remaining eight treaties, five do not contain a provision on associated enterprises at all, which can be clarified by the fact that these treaties only cover cases of certain items of income of individuals, or cover these cases and contain a MAP provision for transfer pricing adjustments. For the remaining three treaties the following analysis is made:

- One treaty contains a provision that is based on Article 9(2) of the OECD Model Tax Convention (OECD, 2017), but the granting of a corresponding adjustment is only optional as the word "shall" instead of "may" and is therefore not being considered the equivalent thereof.

- One treaty contains a provision that is based on Article 9(2) of the OECD Model Tax Convention (OECD, 2017), but it contains an additional phrase under which corresponding adjustments shall be only granted where the competent authorities agree and is therefore not being considered the equivalent thereof.

- One treaty contains a provision that is based on Article 9(2) of the OECD Model Tax Convention (OECD, 2017), but does not contain the last part of the sentence stating that the competent authorities "shall if necessary consult each other".

52.   Access to MAP should be provided in transfer pricing cases regardless of whether the equivalent of Article 9(2) is contained in the Isle of Man's tax treaties and irrespective of whether its domestic legislation enables the granting of corresponding adjustments. In accordance with element B.3, as translated from the Action 14 Minimum Standard, the Isle of Man indicated that it will always provide access to MAP for transfer pricing cases and is willing to make corresponding adjustments, provided that the treaty contains a provision on associated enterprises based on Article 9 of the OECD Model Tax Convention (OECD, 2017).

53.   The MAP guidance of the Isle of Man, under the heading "When can I initiate a MAP", contains examples of cases for which a MAP request can be submitted. These examples also concern transfer pricing cases.

Recent developments

Bilateral modifications

54.   There are no recent developments as to new treaties or amendments to existing treaties being signed in relation to element B.3.

Multilateral Instrument

55.   The Isle of Man reported that it is in favour of including Article 9(2) of the OECD Model Tax Convention (OECD, 2017) in its tax treaties where possible and that it will seek to include this provision in all of its future tax treaties. In that regard, the Isle of Man signed the Multilateral Instrument and deposited its instrument of ratification on 25 October 2017. The Multilateral Instrument for the Isle of Man entered into force on 1 July 2018.

56.   Article 17(2) of that instrument stipulates that Article 17(1) – containing the equivalent of Article 9(2) of the OECD Model Tax Convention (OECD, 2017) – will apply in place of or in the absence of a provision in tax treaties that is equivalent to Article 9(2) of the OECD Model Tax Convention (OECD, 2017). However, this shall only apply if both contracting parties to the applicable tax treaty have listed this treaty as a covered tax agreement under the Multilateral Instrument. Article 17(2) of the Multilateral Instrument does not take effect for a tax treaty if one or both of the treaty partners have, pursuant to Article 17(3), reserved the right not to apply Article 17(2) for those tax treaties that already contain the equivalent of Article 9(2) of the OECD Model Tax Convention (OECD, 2017), or not to apply Article 17(2) in the absence of such equivalent under the condition that: (i) it shall make appropriate corresponding adjustments or (ii) its competent authority shall endeavour to resolve the case under mutual agreement procedure of the applicable tax treaty. Where neither treaty partner has made such a reservation, Article 17(4) of the Multilateral Instrument stipulates that both have to notify the depositary whether the applicable treaty already contains a provision equivalent to Article 9(2) of the OECD Model Tax Convention (OECD, 2017). Where such a notification is made by both of them, the Multilateral Instrument will modify this treaty to replace that provision. If neither or only one treaty partner made this notification, Article 17(1) of the Multilateral Instrument will supersede this treaty only to the extent that the provision contained in that treaty relating to the granting of corresponding adjustments is incompatible with Article 17(1) (containing the equivalent of Article 9(2) of the OECD Model Tax Convention (OECD, 2017)).

57.   The Isle of Man has, pursuant to Article 17(3), reserved the right not to apply Article 17(2) of the Multilateral Instrument for those treaties that already contain a provision equivalent to Article 9(2) of the OECD Model Tax Convention (OECD, 2017). In regard of the three treaties identified in paragraph 51 that are considered not to contain a provision that is equivalent to Article 9(2) of the OECD Model Tax Convention (OECD, 2017; disregarding those five treaties that do not contain Article 9 at all), the Isle of Man listed all of them as a covered tax agreement under the Multilateral Instrument and included one of them in the list of treaties for which the Isle of Man has, pursuant to Article 17(3), reserved the right not to apply Article 17(2) of the Multilateral Instrument. For the remaining treaty the Isle of Man did not make, pursuant to Article 17(4), a notification that this treaty does not contain such equivalent.

58.   The relevant treaty partner is a signatory to the Multilateral Instrument, listed its treaty with the Isle of Man under that instrument, but also, on the basis of Article 17(3), reserved the right not to apply Article 17(2) for its covered tax agreements. Therefore, at this stage, none of the two tax treaties identified above will be modified by the Multilateral Instrument to include the equivalent of Article 9(2) of the OECD Model Tax Convention (OECD, 2017).

Application of legal and administrative framework in practice

Period 1 January 2016-31 March 2019 (stage 1)

59.   The Isle of Man reported that in the period 1 January 2016-31 March 2019, it has not denied access to MAP on the basis that the case concerned a transfer pricing case. However, no such cases in relation hereto were received since that date.

60.   Peers did not provide input in relation to the Isle of Man's implementation of the Action 14 Minimum Standard.

Period 1 April 2019-31 December 2020 (stage 2)

61.   The Isle of Man reported that since 1 April 2019, it has also not received any MAP requests concerning transfer pricing cases and therefore has not denied access to MAP on the basis that the case concerned was a transfer pricing case.

62.   The peer that provided input during stage 2 did not provide input in relation to their tax treaty with the Isle of Man.

Anticipated modifications

63.   The Isle of Man reported that it is in favour of including Article 9(2) of the OECD Model Tax Convention (OECD, 2017) in its tax treaties where possible and that it will seek to include this provision in all of its future tax treaties.

Conclusion

	Areas for improvement	Recommendations
[B.3]	-	-

[B.4]   Provide access to MAP in relation to the application of anti-abuse provisions

> Jurisdictions should provide access to MAP in cases in which there is a disagreement between the taxpayer and the tax authorities making the adjustment as to whether the conditions for the application of a treaty anti-abuse provision have been met or as to whether the application of a domestic law anti-abuse provision is in conflict with the provisions of a treaty.

64.   There is no general rule denying access to MAP in cases of perceived abuse. In order to protect taxpayers from arbitrary application of anti-abuse provisions in tax treaties and in order to ensure that competent authorities have a common understanding on such application, it is important that taxpayers have access to MAP if they consider the interpretation and/or application of a treaty anti-abuse provision as being incorrect. Subsequently, to avoid cases in which the application of domestic anti-abuse legislation is in conflict with the provisions of a tax treaty, it is also important that taxpayers have access to MAP in such cases.

Legal and administrative framework

65.   None of the Isle of Man's 24 tax treaties allow competent authorities to restrict access to MAP for cases where a treaty anti-abuse provision applies or where there is a disagreement between the taxpayer and the tax authorities as to whether the application of a domestic law anti-abuse provision is in conflict with the provisions of a tax treaty. In addition, the domestic law and/or administrative processes of the Isle of Man do not include a provision allowing its competent authority to limit access to MAP for cases in which there is a disagreement between the taxpayer and the tax authorities as to whether the conditions for the application of a domestic law anti-abuse provision is in conflict with the provisions of a tax treaty.

66.   The Isle of Man reported that it will give access to MAP for cases concerning the application of anti-abuse provisions. Its MAP guidance, under the heading "Where can I initiate a MAP", contains a list of examples when a MAP request can be submitted. One of these examples refers to the case where a taxpayer is in disagreement as to whether the conditions for the application of an anti-abuse provision in a tax treaty have been met or

as to whether the application of a domestic law anti-abuse provision is in conflict with the provisions of a tax treaty.

Recent developments

67.   There are no recent developments with respect to element B.4.

Practical application

Period 1 January 2016-31 March 2019 (stage 1)

68.   The Isle of Man reported that in the period 1 January 2016-31 March 2019 it has not denied access to MAP in cases in which there was a disagreement between the taxpayer and the tax authorities as to whether the conditions for the application of a treaty anti-abuse provision have been met, or as to whether the application of a domestic law anti-abuse provision is in conflict with the provisions of a tax treaty. However, no such cases in relation hereto were received since that date.

69.   Peers did not provide input in relation to the Isle of Man's implementation of the Action 14 Minimum Standard.

Period 1 April 2019-31 December 2020 (stage 2)

70.   The Isle of Man reported that since 1 April 2019 it has also not denied access to MAP in cases in which there was a disagreement between the taxpayer and the tax authorities as to whether the conditions for the application of a treaty anti-abuse provision have been met, or as to whether the application of a domestic law anti-abuse provision is in conflict with the provisions of a tax treaty. However, no such cases in relation hereto were received since that date.

71.   The peer that provided input during stage 2 did not provide input in relation to element B.4.

Anticipated modifications

72.   The Isle of Man did not indicate that it anticipates any modifications in relation to element B.4.

Conclusion

	Areas for improvement	Recommendations
[B.4]	-	-

[B.5] Provide access to MAP in cases of audit settlements

> Jurisdictions should not deny access to MAP in cases where there is an audit settlement between tax authorities and taxpayers. If jurisdictions have an administrative or statutory dispute settlement/resolution process independent from the audit and examination functions and that can only be accessed through a request by the taxpayer, jurisdictions may limit access to the MAP with respect to the matters resolved through that process.

73.   An audit settlement procedure can be valuable to taxpayers by providing certainty on their tax position. Nevertheless, as double taxation may not be fully eliminated by agreeing on such settlements, taxpayers should have access to the MAP in such cases, unless they were already resolved via an administrative or statutory disputes settlement/resolution process that functions independently from the audit and examination function and which is only accessible through a request by taxpayers.

Legal and administrative framework

Audit settlements

74.   The Isle of Man reported that it is possible that the taxpayer and the tax administration enter into an audit settlement during the course of or after an audit has been finalised. The Isle of Man explained that the tax administration can issue an assessment it if is of the opinion that the tax return does not reflect the correct amount of income. During the assessment process, the correct taxation of income would be discussed with the taxpayer. If the validity of the adjustment and/or the amount of double taxation relief would be agreed between the taxpayer and the tax administration, then the adjustment would be incorporated in the tax assessment.

75.   The Isle of Man further reported that entering into an audit settlement would not preclude taxpayers from access to MAP. In this respect, the MAP guidance of the Isle of Man, under the heading "When can I initiate a MAP", stipulates that the taxpayer will not be precluded from using the MAP simply because the taxpayer and the tax administration entered into an audit settlement.

Administrative or statutory dispute settlement/resolution process

76.   The Isle of Man reported it does not have an administrative or statutory dispute settlement/resolution process in place, which is independent from the audit and examination functions and which can only be accessed through a request by the taxpayer.

Recent developments

77.   There are no recent developments with respect to element B.5.

Practical application

Period 1 January 2016-31 March 2019 (stage 1)

78.   The Isle of Man reported that in the period 1 January 2016-31 March 2019 it had not denied access to MAP for cases where the issue presented by the taxpayer has already been dealt with in an audit settlement between the taxpayer and the tax administration. However, no such cases in relation hereto were received since that date.

79.   Peers did not provide input in relation to the Isle of Man's implementation of the Action 14 Minimum Standard.

Period 1 April 2019-31 December 2020 (stage 2)

80.   The Isle of Man reported that since 1 April 2019 it has also not denied access to MAP for cases where the issue presented by the taxpayer in a MAP request had already been resolved through an audit settlement between the taxpayer and the tax administration. However, no such cases in relation hereto were received since that date.

81.   The peer that provided input during stage 2 did not provide input in relation to element B.5.

Anticipated modifications

82.   The Isle of Man did not indicate that it anticipates any modifications in relation to element B.5.

Conclusion

	Areas for improvement	Recommendations
[B.5]	-	-

[B.6] Provide access to MAP if required information is submitted

> Jurisdictions should not limit access to MAP based on the argument that insufficient information was provided if the taxpayer has provided the required information based on the rules, guidelines and procedures made available to taxpayers on access to and the use of MAP.

83.   To resolve cases where there is taxation not in accordance with the provisions of the tax treaty, it is important that competent authorities do not limit access to MAP when taxpayers have complied with the information and documentation requirements as provided in the jurisdiction's guidance relating hereto. Access to MAP will be facilitated when such required information and documentation is made publicly available.

Legal framework on access to MAP and information to be submitted

84.   The information and documentation the Isle of Man requires taxpayers to include in a request for MAP assistance are discussed under element B.8.

85.   The Isle of Man reported that when taxpayers do not include in their MAP request all the required information pursuant to their MAP guidance, additional information will be requested. There, however, is no standard timeframe for submission of additional requested information. Given the very limited number of MAP cases the Isle of Man receives, it would in practice contact the taxpayer to request additional information and discuss with the taxpayer the time required to submit such information.

Recent developments

86.   There are no recent developments with respect to element B.6.

Practical application

Period 1 January 2016-31 March 2019 (stage 1)

87.   The Isle of Man reported that it provides access to MAP in all cases where taxpayers have complied with the information or documentation requirements as set out in its MAP guidance. It further reported that in the period 1 January 2016-31 March 2019, it has not received any MAP request from taxpayers.

88.   Peers provided no specific input in relation to element B.6.

Period 1 April 2019-31 December 2020 (stage 2)

89.   The Isle of Man reported that since 1 April 2019 it has also not denied access to MAP for cases where the taxpayer had not provided the required information or documentation.

90.   The peer that provided input during stage 2 did not provide input in relation to element B.6.

Anticipated modifications

91.   The Isle of Man did not indicate that it anticipates any modifications in relation to element B.6.

Conclusion

	Areas for improvement	Recommendations
[B.6]	-	-

[B.7] Include Article 25(3), second sentence, of the OECD Model Tax Convention in tax treaties

> Jurisdictions should ensure that their tax treaties contain a provision under which competent authorities may consult together for the elimination of double taxation in cases not provided for in their tax treaties.

92.   For ensuring that tax treaties operate effectively and in order for competent authorities to be able to respond quickly to unanticipated situations, it is useful that tax treaties include the second sentence of Article 25(3) of the OECD Model Tax Convention (OECD, 2017), enabling them to consult together for the elimination of double taxation in cases not provided for by these treaties.

Current situation of the Isle of Man's tax treaties

93.   Out of the Isle of Man's 24 tax treaties, 11 contain a provision that is equivalent to Article 25(3), second sentence, of the OECD Model Tax Convention (OECD, 2017) allowing their competent authorities to consult together for the elimination of double taxation in cases not provided for in their tax treaties. The remaining 13 tax treaties doe not contain a provision that is based on or the equivalent of Article 25(3), second sentence, of the OECD Model Tax Convention (OECD, 2017).

94.   For 12 of these 13 tax treaties this can be clarified by the fact that they have a limited scope of application. This concerns tax treaties that only apply to a certain category of income or a certain category of taxpayers, whereby the structure and articles of the OECD Model Tax Convention (OECD, 2017) are not followed. As these treaties were intentionally negotiated with a limited scope, the inclusion of Article 25(3), second sentence, of the OECD Model Tax Convention (OECD, 2017) would contradict the object and purpose of those treaties and such inclusion would also be inappropriate, as it would allow competent authorities the possibility to consult in cases that have intentionally been excluded from the scope of a tax treaty. For this reason, therefore, there is a justification not to contain Article 25(3), second sentence, of the OECD Model Tax Convention (OECD, 2017) for those 12 treaties with a limited scope of application.

95.   One peer provided input during stage 1 and mentioned that its treaty with the Isle of Man is a treaty with a limited scope that applies to a narrower range of circumstances than the MAP articles contained in comprehensive tax treaties. The peer further reported that it has not sought to amend its MAP article in order to meet the requirements under the Action 14 minimum standard. It also did not indicate it was contacted by the Isle of Man for this purpose.

Recent developments

Bilateral modifications

96.   There are no recent developments as to new treaties or amendments to existing treaties being signed in relation to element B.7.

Multilateral Instrument

97.   The Isle of Man signed the Multilateral Instrument and deposited its instrument of ratification on 25 October 2017. The Multilateral Instrument for the Isle of Man entered into force on 1 July 2018.

98.   Article 16(4)(c)(ii) of that instrument stipulates that Article 16(3), second sentence – containing the equivalent of Article 25(3), second sentence, of the OECD Model Tax Convention (OECD, 2017) – will apply in the absence of a provision in tax treaties that is equivalent to Article 25(3), second sentence, of the OECD Model Tax Convention (OECD, 2017). In other words, in the absence of this equivalent, Article 16(4)(c)(ii) of the Multilateral Instrument will modify the applicable tax treaty to include such equivalent. However, this shall only apply if both contracting parties to the applicable tax treaty have listed this treaty as a covered tax agreement under the Multilateral Instrument and insofar as both notified, pursuant to Article 16(6)(d)(ii), the depositary that this treaty does not contain the equivalent of Article 25(3), second sentence, of the OECD Model Tax Convention (OECD, 2017).

99.   As 12 of the 13 treaties identified above that do not contain the equivalent of Article 25(3), second sentence, of the OECD Model Tax Convention (OECD, 2017), have a limited scope of application, no modifications are necessary in order to be in line with element B.7. In regard of the remaining comprehensive tax treaty, the Isle of Man listed this treaty as a covered tax agreement under the Multilateral Instrument and made, pursuant to Article 16(6)(d)(ii), a notification that it does not contain a provision described in Article 16(4)(c)(ii). The relevant treaty partner, being a signatory to the Multilateral Instrument, listed the treaty with the Isle of Man as a covered tax agreement and also made

such notification. This treaty partner has already deposited its instrument of ratification of the Multilateral Instrument, following which the Multilateral Instrument has entered into force for the treaty between the Isle of Man and this treaty partner, and therefore has modified this treaty to include the equivalent of Article 25(3), second sentence, of the OECD Model Tax Convention (OECD, 2017).

Peer input

100.   The peer that provided input during stage 2 did not provide input in relation to their tax treaty with the Isle of Man.

Anticipated modifications

101.   The Isle of Man reported it will seek to include Article 25(3), first sentence, of the OECD Model Tax Convention (OECD, 2017) in all of its future tax treaties.

Conclusion

	Areas for improvement	Recommendations
[B.7]	-	-

[B.8] Publish clear and comprehensive MAP guidance

> Jurisdictions should publish clear rules, guidelines and procedures on access to and use of the MAP and include the specific information and documentation that should be submitted in a taxpayer's request for MAP assistance.

102.   Information on a jurisdiction's MAP regime facilitates the timely initiation and resolution of MAP cases. Clear rules, guidelines and procedures on access to and use of the MAP are essential for making taxpayers and other stakeholders aware of how a jurisdiction's MAP regime functions. In addition, to ensure that a MAP request is received and will be reviewed by the competent authority in a timely manner, it is important that a jurisdiction's MAP guidance clearly and comprehensively explains how a taxpayer can make a MAP request and what information and documentation should be included in such request.

The Isle of Man's MAP guidance

103.   The Isle of Man's has published rules, guidelines and procedures in Guidance Note – GN 57 ("**MAP guidance**"). This guidance was issued on 28 February 2019 and was last updated in December 2020, and is available at:

https://www.gov.im/media/1364504/gn-57-map-guide-december-2020-update.pdf

104.   The MAP guidance sets out in detail how taxpayers can access the mutual agreement procedure and what rules apply during that procedure under tax treaties the Isle of Man entered into, and is divided into 12 sections titled as follows:

105.   This document includes information on:

a.   contact information of the competent authority or the office in charge of MAP cases

b.   the manner and form in which the taxpayer should submit its MAP request

c.   the specific information and documentation that should be included in a MAP request (see also below)

d.   how the MAP functions in terms of timing and the role of the competent authorities

e.   information on availability of arbitration

f.   Access to MAP in transfer pricing cases, cases concerning the application of anti-abuse provisions, and in cases where taxpayers and the tax administration have already entered into an audit settlement, multilateral disputes, bona fide foreign-initiated self-adjustments and for multi-year resolution of cases

g.   implementation of MAP agreements

h.   rights and role of taxpayers in the process

i.   suspension of tax collection during the period a MAP case is pending

j.   interest charges and penalties.

106.   The above-described MAP guidance of the Isle of Man contains detailed information on the availability and the use of MAP and how its competent authority conducts the procedure in practice. This guidance includes the information that the FTA MAP Forum agreed should be included in a jurisdiction's MAP guidance, which concerns: (i) contact information of the competent authority or the office in charge of MAP cases and (ii) the manner and form in which the taxpayer should submit its MAP request.[2]

107.   While the information included in the Isle of Man's MAP guidance is detailed, information on relationship with domestic available remedies is not specifically discussed in the Isle of Man's MAP guidance.

Information and documentation to be included in a MAP request

108.   To facilitate the review of a MAP request by competent authorities and to have more consistency in the required content of MAP requests, the FTA MAP Forum agreed on guidance that jurisdictions could use in their domestic guidance on what information and documentation taxpayers need to include in request for MAP assistance.[3] This agreed

guidance is shown below. The Isle of Man's MAP guidance enumerating which items must be included in a request for MAP assistance are checked in the following list:

- ☑ identity of the taxpayer(s) covered in the MAP request

- ☑ the basis for the request

- ☑ facts of the case

- ☑ analysis of the issue(s) requested to be resolved via MAP

- ☑ whether the MAP request was also submitted to the competent authority of the other treaty partner

- ☑ whether the MAP request was also submitted to another authority under another instrument that provides for a mechanism to resolve treaty-related disputes

- ☑ whether the issue(s) involved were dealt with previously

- ☐ a statement confirming that all information and documentation provided in the MAP request is accurate and that the taxpayer will assist the competent authority in its resolution of the issue(s) presented in the MAP request by furnishing any other information or documentation required by the competent authority in a timely manner.

109.   Further to the above, the Isle of Man's MAP guidance also requires taxpayers to provide in their MAP request: (i) contact details of the other tax administration and competent authorities concerned, (ii) the fiscal years involved, (iii) a possible copy of a settlement agreement with the other jurisdiction concerned and (iv) for transfer pricing cases: copies of relevant documentation.

Recent developments

110.   The Isle of Man reported that it has updated its MAP guidance in December 2020 to include information that was suggested in its stage 1 report. This concerns:

- whether MAP is available in cases of: (i) multilateral disputes and (ii) bona fide foreign-initiated self-adjustments

- whether taxpayers can request for the multi-year resolution of recurring issues through MAP

- the possibility of suspension of tax collection during the course of a MAP

- the consideration of interest and penalties in MAP

- the steps of the process and the timing of such steps for the implementation of MAP agreements, including any actions to be taken by taxpayers (if any).

111.   This update has been reflected in the above analysis.

Anticipated modifications

112.   The Isle of Man did not indicate that it anticipates any modifications in relation to element B.8.

Conclusion

	Areas for improvement	Recommendations
[B.8]	-	-

[B.9] Make MAP guidance available and easily accessible and publish MAP profile

> Jurisdictions should take appropriate measures to make rules, guidelines and procedures on access to and use of the MAP available and easily accessible to the public and should publish their jurisdiction MAP profiles on a shared public platform pursuant to the agreed template.

113. The public availability and accessibility of a jurisdiction's MAP guidance increases public awareness on access to and the use of the MAP in that jurisdiction. Publishing MAP profiles on a shared public platform further promotes the transparency and dissemination of the MAP programme.[4]

Rules, guidelines and procedures on access to and use of the MAP

114. The MAP guidance of the Isle of Man is published and can be found at:

https://www.gov.im/media/1364504/gn-57-map-guide-december-2020-update.pdf

115. This guidance was introduced in February 2019 and updated in December 2020. As regards its accessibility, the Isle of Man's MAP guidance can easily be found on the website of the government of the Isle of Man by searching for e.g. "MAP".

MAP profile

116. The MAP profile of the Isle of Man is published on the website of the OECD and was last updated in May 2021.[5] This MAP profile is complete and often with detailed information. This profile includes external links that provide extra information and guidance where appropriate.

Recent developments

117. The Isle of Man reported that it has updated its MAP profile following the update of its MAP guidance.

Anticipated modifications

118. The Isle of Man did not indicate that it anticipates any modifications in relation to element B.9.

Conclusion

	Areas for improvement	Recommendations
[B.9]	-	-

[B.10] Clarify in MAP guidance that audit settlements do not preclude access to MAP

> Jurisdictions should clarify in their MAP guidance that audit settlements between tax authorities and taxpayers do not preclude access to MAP. If jurisdictions have an administrative or statutory dispute settlement/resolution process independent from the audit and examination functions and that can only be accessed through a request by the taxpayer, and jurisdictions limit access to the MAP with respect to the matters resolved through that process, jurisdictions should notify their treaty partners of such administrative or statutory processes and should expressly address the effects of those processes with respect to the MAP in their public guidance on such processes and in their public MAP programme guidance.

119. As explained under element B.5, an audit settlement can be valuable to taxpayers by providing certainty to them on their tax position. Nevertheless, as double taxation may not be fully eliminated by agreeing with such settlements, it is important that a jurisdiction's MAP guidance clarifies that in case of audit settlement taxpayers have access to the MAP. In addition, for providing clarity on the relationship between administrative or statutory dispute settlement or resolution processes and the MAP (if any), it is critical that both the public guidance on such processes and the public MAP programme guidance address the effects of those processes, if any. Finally, as the MAP represents a collaborative approach between treaty partners, it is helpful that treaty partners are notified of each other's MAP programme and limitations thereto, particularly in relation to the previously mentioned processes.

MAP and audit settlements in the MAP guidance

120. As previously discussed under B.5, under the Isle of Man's domestic law it is possible that taxpayers and the tax administration enter into audit settlements. The relationship between access to MAP and audit settlements is described in the Isle of Man's MAP guidance, under the heading "When can I initiate a MAP", It is there explicitly stated that taxpayers will not be precluded from using the MAP procedure simply because the taxpayer had already entered into audit settlements.

121. Peers did not provide input in relation to the Isle of Man's implementation of the Action 14 Minimum Standard.

MAP and other administrative or statutory dispute settlement/resolution processes in available guidance

122. As previously mentioned under element B.5, the Isle of Man does not have an administrative or statutory dispute settlement/resolution process in place that is independent from the audit and examination functions and that can only be accessed through a request by the taxpayer. In that regard, there is no need to address the effects of such process with respect to MAP in the Isle of Man's MAP guidance.

Notification of treaty partners of existing administrative or statutory dispute settlement/resolution processes

123. As the Isle of Man does not have an internal administrative or statutory dispute settlement/resolution process in place, there is no need for notifying treaty partners of such process.

Recent developments

124. There are no recent developments with respect to element B.10.

Anticipated modifications

125. The Isle of Man did not indicate that it anticipates any modifications in relation to element B.10.

Conclusion

	Areas for improvement	Recommendations
[B.10]	-	-

Notes

1. Seven of these 16 treaties concern treaties with a limited scope that either only contain a provision on associated enterprises or cover cases of certain items of income of individuals and a provision on associated enterprises.

2. Available at: www.oecd.org/tax/beps/beps-action-14-on-more-effective-dispute-resolution-peer-review-documents.pdf.

3. Ibid.

4. The shared public platform can be found at: www.oecd.org/ctp/dispute/country-map-profiles.htm.

5. Available at: www.oecd.org/tax/dispute/Isle-of-Man-Dispute-Resolution-Profile.pdf.

References

OECD (2015a), *Model Tax Convention on Income and on Capital 2014 (Full Version)*, OECD Publishing, Paris, https://dx.doi.org/10.1787/9789264239081-en.

OECD (2015b), "Making Dispute Resolution Mechanisms More Effective, Action 14 – 2015 Final Report", in *OECD/G20 Base Erosion and Profit Shifting Project*, OECD Publishing, Paris, https://dx.doi.org/10.1787/9789264241633-en.

OECD (2017), *Model Tax Convention on Income and on Capital 2017 (Full Version)*, OECD Publishing, Paris, https://dx.doi.org/10.1787/g2g972ee-en.

Part C

Resolution of MAP cases

[C.1] Include Article 25(2), first sentence, of the OECD Model Tax Convention in tax treaties

> Jurisdictions should ensure that their tax treaties contain a provision which requires that the competent authority who receives a MAP request from the taxpayer, shall endeavour, if the objection from the taxpayer appears to be justified and the competent authority is not itself able to arrive at a satisfactory solution, to resolve the MAP case by mutual agreement with the competent authority of the other Contracting Party, with a view to the avoidance of taxation which is not in accordance with the tax treaty.

126.   It is of critical importance that in addition to allowing taxpayers to request for a MAP, tax treaties also include the equivalent of the first sentence of Article 25(2) of the OECD Model Tax Convention (OECD, 2017), which obliges competent authorities, in situations where the objection raised by taxpayers are considered justified and where cases cannot be unilaterally resolved, to enter into discussions with each other to resolve cases of taxation not in accordance with the provisions of a tax treaty.

Current situation of the Isle of Man's tax treaties

127.   Out of the Isle of Man's 24 tax treaties, 21 contain a provision equivalent to Article 25(2), first sentence, of the OECD Model Tax Convention (OECD, 2017) requiring its competent authority to endeavour – when the objection raised is considered justified and no unilateral solution is possible – to resolve by mutual agreement with the competent authority of the other treaty partner the MAP case with a view to the avoidance of taxation which is not in accordance with the tax treaty. Out of the remaining three treaties, two do not contain such provision at all. The remaining treaty contains a provision that is based on Article 25(2), first sentence, of the OECD Model Tax Convention (OECD, 2017), but the phrase "with a view to the avoidance of taxation which is not in accordance with the Convention" is missing. Therefore, this treaty is considered as not being equivalent to Article 25(2), first sentence, of the OECD Model Tax Convention (OECD, 2017).

128.   One peer provided input during stage 1 and mentioned that its treaty with the Isle of Man is a treaty with a limited scope that applies to a narrower range of circumstances than the MAP articles contained in comprehensive tax treaties. The peer further reported that it has not sought to amend its MAP article in order to meet the requirements under the Action 14 minimum standard. It also did not indicate it was contacted by the Isle of Man for this purpose.

Recent developments

Bilateral modifications

129.   There are no recent developments as to new treaties or amendments to existing treaties being signed in relation to element C.1.

Multilateral Instrument

130.   The Isle of Man signed the Multilateral Instrument and deposited its instrument of ratification on 25 October 2017. The Multilateral Instrument for the Isle of Man entered into force on 1 July 2018.

131.   Article 16(4)(b)(i) of that instrument stipulates that Article 16(2), first sentence – containing the equivalent of Article 25(2), first sentence, of the OECD Model Tax Convention (OECD, 2017) – will apply in the absence of a provision in tax treaties that is equivalent to Article 25(2), first sentence, of the OECD Model Tax Convention (OECD, 2017). In other words, in the absence of this equivalent, Article 16(4)(b)(i) of the Multilateral Instrument will modify the applicable tax treaty to include such equivalent. However, this shall only apply if both contracting parties to the applicable tax treaty have listed this treaty as a covered tax agreement under the Multilateral Instrument and insofar as both notified, pursuant to Article 16(6)(c)(i), the depositary that this treaty does not contain the equivalent of Article 25(2), first sentence, of the OECD Model Tax Convention (OECD, 2017).

132.   In regard of the three tax treaties identified above that are considered not to contain the equivalent of Article 25(2), first sentence, of the OECD Model Tax Convention (OECD, 2017), the Isle of Man listed none of them as a covered tax agreement under the Multilateral Instrument. Therefore, at this stage, none of the three tax treaties will be modified by the Multilateral Instrument to include the equivalent of Article 25(2), first sentence, of the OECD Model Tax Convention (OECD, 2017).

Other developments

133.   The Isle of Man reported that for one of the three tax treaties that do not contain the equivalent of Article 25(2), first sentence, of the OECD Model Tax Convention (OECD, 2017) and that will not be modified by the Multilateral Instrument, negotiations were finalised on an amending protocol to the existing treaty.

Peer input

134.   The peer that provided input during stage 2 did not provide input in relation to their tax treaty with the Isle of Man.

Anticipated modifications

135.   The Isle of Man reported that for the remaining two tax treaties that do not contain the equivalent of Article 25(2), first sentence, of the OECD Model Tax Convention (OECD, 2017) and that will not be modified by the Multilateral Instrument, it is awaiting a response from the treaty partners to its request of the initiation of bilateral negotiations to amend the treaties to meet the requirements under the Action 14 Minimum Standard.

136.   The Isle of Man reported it will seek to include Article 25(2), first sentence, of the OECD Model Tax Convention (OECD, 2017) in all of its future tax treaties.

Conclusion

	Areas for improvement	Recommendations
[C.1]	Three out of 24 tax treaties do not contain a provision that is equivalent to Article 25(2), first sentence, of the OECD Model Tax Convention (OECD, 2017). None of these treaties will be modified by the Multilateral Instrument to include the required provision. With respect to these three treaties: • The Isle of Man has reached out to two treaty partners to request the initiation of bilateral negotiations, for which it is awaiting a response. • For one, negotiations were finalised.	For two of the three treaties that do not contain the equivalent of Article 25(2), first sentence, of the OECD Model Tax Convention (OECD, 2017) and will not be modified via the Multilateral Instrument, the Isle of Man should, upon receipt of a response from the relevant treaty partners agreeing to include the required provision, work towards updating the treaties to include this provision. Furthermore, for the third treaty, the Isle of Man should as quickly as possible sign and ratify the amending protocol to have in place the required provision.

[C.2] Seek to resolve MAP cases within a 24-month average timeframe

> Jurisdictions should seek to resolve MAP cases within an average time frame of 24 months. This time frame applies to both jurisdictions (i.e. the jurisdiction which receives the MAP request from the taxpayer and its treaty partner).

137.   As double taxation creates uncertainties and leads to costs for both taxpayers and jurisdictions, and as the resolution of MAP cases may also avoid (potential) similar issues for future years concerning the same taxpayers, it is important that MAP cases are resolved swiftly. A period of 24 months is considered as an appropriate time period to resolve MAP cases on average.

Reporting of MAP statistics

138.   Statistics regarding all tax treaty related disputes concerning the Isle of Man are published on the website of the OECD as of 2016.[1]

139.   The FTA MAP Forum has agreed on rules for reporting of MAP statistics ("**MAP Statistics Reporting Framework**") for MAP requests submitted on or after 1 January 2016 "**post-2015 cases**"). Also, for MAP requests submitted prior to that date ("**pre-2016 cases**"), the FTA MAP Forum agreed to report MAP statistics on the basis of an agreed template. The Isle of Man provided its MAP statistics pursuant to the MAP Statistics Reporting Framework within the given deadline, including all cases involving the Isle of Man and of which its competent authority was aware. The statistics discussed below include both pre-2016 and post-2015 cases and the full statistics are attached to this report as Annex B and Annex C respectively[2] and should be considered jointly to understand the MAP caseload of the Isle of Man.

140.   With respect to post-2015 cases, the Isle of Man reported it had only one MAP case throughout the Statistics Reporting Period, which started in 2018 and was closed in 2019. For this case, the Isle of Man reported that it has reached out to the MAP partner with a view to have its MAP statistics matching, and it could match the statistics.

Monitoring of MAP statistics

141.   The Isle of Man reported that although it has very limited MAP caseload, it has prepared a spreadsheet to monitor the inventory, new requests and resolution times of future MAP cases. In that regard, the MAP guidance of the Isle of Man, under the heading "How long do MAP cases take to resolve", it is stated that its competent authority aims at resolving MAP cases within a period of two years.

Analysis of the Isle of Man's MAP caseload

142. The analysis of the Isle of Man's MAP caseload relates to the period starting on 1 January 2016 and ending on 31 December 2020.[3]

143. Figure C.1 shows the evolution of the Isle of Man's MAP caseload over the Statistics Reporting Period.

Figure C.1. **Evolution of the Isle of Man's MAP caseload**

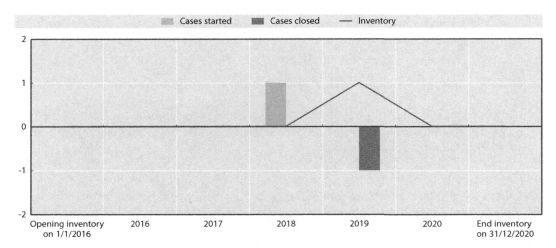

144. During the Statistics Reporting Period, one non-attribution/allocation case started in 2018 and was closed in 2019. Therefore, there is no MAP case in the Isle of Man's end inventory.

Pre-2016 cases

145. The Isle of Man did not have any pre-2016 cases during the Statistics Reporting Period.

Post-2015 cases

146. As mentioned above, the Isle of Man had one case that started in 2018 and that was closed in 2019. This concerns an other case.

Overview of cases closed during the Statistics Reporting Period

Reported outcomes

147. During the Statistical Reporting Period, the Isle of Man closed one other post-2015 MAP case with the outcome "agreement fully eliminating double taxation/fully resolving taxation not in accordance with tax treaty".

Average timeframe needed to resolve MAP cases

All cases closed during the Statistics Reporting Period

148.   The time needed to close one MAP case during the Statistics Reporting Period was 13.55 months. It is shown as follows:

	Number of cases	Start date to End date (in months)
Attribution/Allocation cases	0	N/A
Other cases	1	13.55
All cases	1	13.55

Peer input

149.   Peers did not provide input during stage 1 in relation to the Isle of Man's implementation of the Action 14 Minimum Standard.

Recent developments

150.   In the stage 1 peer review report of the Isle of Man, it was concluded that as there was only one post-2015 MAP case in the inventory, which was still pending at that time, it was not possible to evaluate whether the Isle of Man's competent authority seeks to resolve MAP cases within an average time frame of 24 months.

151.   With respect to this conclusion, the Isle of Man reported that it closed the post-2015 MAP case within 24 months, and it will seek to resolve future MAP cases within an average timeframe of 24 months.

152.   From the statistics discussed above, it follows that the Isle of Man has in the period 2016-20 closed one MAP case within the pursued average of 24 months. For these years, as discussed above, the Isle of Man had only one case that started in 2018 and was closed in 2019, and therefore there is no MAP case in the Isle of Man's end inventory.

153.   The peer that provided input during stage 2 did not provide input in relation to element C.2.

Anticipated modifications

154.   The Isle of Man did not indicate that it anticipates any modifications in relation to element C.2.

Conclusion

	Areas for improvement	Recommendations
[C.2]	-	-

[C.3] Provide adequate resources to the MAP function

Jurisdictions should ensure that adequate resources are provided to the MAP function.

155. Adequate resources, including personnel, funding and training, are necessary to properly perform the competent authority function and to ensure that MAP cases are resolved in a timely, efficient and effective manner.

Description of the Isle of Man's competent authority

156. Under the tax treaties the Isle of Man entered into, the competent authority function is assigned to the Assessor of Income Tax, which is the head of the tax administration. This is also reflected in the Isle of Man's MAP guidance. In that regard, giving the very few number of MAP cases it receives, the Isle of Man noted that it has not established a separate MAP team. In practice, a Deputy Assessor who has many years' experience of income tax legislation and double tax agreements handles MAP cases.

157. Concerning the process to handle MAP cases, the Isle of Man reported that when a MAP request is received, it will first analyse whether the request was timely filed and whether it is complete, as also whether the request is valid and whether a unilateral solution is possible. If the conditions are fulfilled and such unilateral solution is not possible, the bilateral phase of the MAP process is initiated. In that situation, staff in charge of MAP has to take into account the following items:

- the text of the applicable tax treaty and the Commentary to the OECD Model Tax Convention (OECD, 2017)

- the position of the Isle of Man in relation to previous MAP cases involving the article and taxation in question

- information published by the other jurisdiction in relation to agreed MAP cases involving the article and taxation in question.

158. The Isle of Man's MAP guidance, under the heading "Our service commitment to you" further stipulates that its competent authority aims to be consistent and reciprocal in the positions they take in handling and resolving MAP cases, thereby not changing its position for each cases dependent on which side of the issue produces the most revenue.

159. With respect to the process to resolve MAP cases and to enter into agreements with other competent authorities, the Isle of Man reported that the competent authority has the authority to enter into such agreements and does not need to request approval from any other government agency.

Monitoring mechanism

160. The Isle of Man reported that it will monitor the number of new MAP cases to evaluate the need for additional resources and funding for MAP. If so, there would be two more deputy assessors who could handle MAP cases if there is an increase in such numbers. The Isle of Man reported that it considers the current resource is sufficient since it deals with very few MAP cases.

Recent development

161. There are no recent developments with respect to element C.3.

Practical application

MAP statistics

162.   As discussed under element C.2, during the Statistics Reporting Period, the Isle of Man closed one MAP case within the pursued 24-months average. The case concerned another post-2015 case and was closed within 13.55 months.

Peer input

163.   Peers did not provide input in relation to the Isle of Man's implementation of the Action 14 Minimum Standard during stage 1 (1 January 2016-31 March 2019) and stage 2 (1 April 2019-31 December 2020).

Anticipated modifications

164.   The Isle of Man did not indicate that it anticipates any modifications in relation to element C.3.

Conclusion

	Areas for improvement	Recommendations
[C.3]	-	-

[C.4]   Ensure staff in charge of MAP has the authority to resolve cases in accordance with the applicable tax treaty

> Jurisdictions should ensure that the staff in charge of MAP processes have the authority to resolve MAP cases in accordance with the terms of the applicable tax treaty, in particular without being dependent on the approval or the direction of the tax administration personnel who made the adjustments at issue or being influenced by considerations of the policy that the jurisdictions would like to see reflected in future amendments to the treaty.

165.   Ensuring that staff in charge of MAP can and will resolve cases, absent any approval/direction by the tax administration personnel directly involved in the adjustment and absent any policy considerations, contributes to a principled and consistent approach to MAP cases.

Functioning of staff in charge of MAP

166.   The Isle of Man reported that in the process of handling and resolving MAP cases, staff in charge of MAP it will liaise with the relevant department within the tax administration to review the facts of the case as presented by the taxpayer and as available to the tax officer when charging the tax in question. In that regard, the Isle of Man clarified that such officer is expected to give regard to the policy aspects of the applicable tax treaty as well as the facts of the case in question in the normal course of the work. Direct consultations with these tax officers will only be required where the basis for the taxation is not clear from the records, or where the competent authority has a different opinion of those facts or the policy applied. To this the Isle of Man added that the Deputy Assessor who is in charge of MAP cases does not deal with day-to-day technical decisions involving cross border taxation issues within the tax administration and operates independently of the main technical teams.

167. In regard of the above, the Isle of Man reported that staff in charge of MAP in practices operates independently and has the authority to resolve MAP cases without being dependent on the approval/direction of the tax administration personnel directly involved in the adjustment and the process for negotiating MAP agreements is not influenced by policy considerations. In this respect, the Isle of Man's MAP guidance, under the heading "Our service commitment to you" further stipulates that its competent authority will engage in discussions with other competent authorities in a principled, fair and objective manner, with each case being decided on its own merits and not by reference to any balance of results in other cases.

Recent developments

168. There are no recent developments with respect to element C.4.

Practical application

169. Peers did not provide input in relation to the Isle of Man's implementation of the Action 14 Minimum Standard during stage 1 (1 January 2016-31 March 2019) and stage 2 (1 April 2019-31 December 2020).

Anticipated modifications

170. The Isle of Man did not indicate that it anticipates any modifications in relation to element C.4.

Conclusion

	Areas for improvement	Recommendations
[C.4]	-	-

[C.5] Use appropriate performance indicators for the MAP function

> Jurisdictions should not use performance indicators for their competent authority functions and staff in charge of MAP processes based on the amount of sustained audit adjustments or maintaining tax revenue.

171. For ensuring that each case is considered on its individual merits and will be resolved in a principled and consistent manner, it is essential that any performance indicators for the competent authority function and for the staff in charge of MAP processes are appropriate and not based on the amount of sustained audit adjustments or aim at maintaining a certain amount of tax revenue.

Performance indicators used by the Isle of Man

172. With regard to the evaluation of the performance of personnel in charge of MAP cases, the Isle of Man reported that its government has a performance appraisal system in place. This system measures personal performance against specific work objectives and development, under which managers are required to meet with their staff six times per year to discuss performance, targets and development. Targets for an individual officer that originate from the Divisions' Group Plan are agreed between line managers and are monitored by the managers.

173.   The Action 14 final report (OECD, 2015) includes examples of performance indicators that are considered appropriate. These indicators are shown below:

- number of MAP cases resolved

- consistency (i.e. a treaty should be applied in a principled and consistent manner to MAP cases involving the same facts and similarly-situated taxpayers)

- time taken to resolve a MAP case (recognising that the time taken to resolve a MAP case may vary according to its complexity and that matters not under the control of a competent authority may have a significant impact on the time needed to resolve a case).

174.   The Isle of Man reported that since it does not have a separate MAP office, there are no performance indicators set for staff in charge of MAP cases. It also reported that it does not use any performance indicators for staff in charge of MAP that are related to the outcome of MAP discussions in terms of the amount of sustained audit adjustments or maintained tax revenue. In other words, staff in charge of MAP is not evaluated on the basis of the material outcome of MAP discussions. In this respect, the Isle of Man's MAP guidance, under the heading "Our service commitment to you" further stipulates that it does not use performance indicators for staff in charge of MAP processes based on the amount of adjustments or tax revenue arising from dealing with MAP cases.

Recent developments

175.   There are no recent developments with respect to element C.5.

Practical application

176.   Peers did not provide input in relation to the Isle of Man's implementation of the Action 14 Minimum Standard during stage 1 (1 January 2016-31 March 2019) and stage 2 (1 April 2019-31 December 2020).

Anticipated modifications

177.   The Isle of Man did not indicate that it anticipates any modifications in relation to element C.5.

Conclusion

	Areas for improvement	Recommendations
[C.5]	-	-

[C.6] Provide transparency with respect to the position on MAP arbitration

> Jurisdictions should provide transparency with respect to their positions on MAP arbitration.

178.   The inclusion of an arbitration provision in tax treaties may help ensure that MAP cases are resolved within a certain timeframe, which provides certainty to both taxpayers and competent authorities. In order to have full clarity on whether arbitration as a final stage in the MAP process can and will be available in jurisdictions it is important that jurisdictions are transparent on their position on MAP arbitration.

Position on MAP arbitration

179. The Isle of Man reported that it has no domestic law limitations for including MAP arbitration in its tax treaties. Its tax treaty policy is to include a mandatory and binding arbitration provision based on Article 25(5) of the OECD Model Tax Convention (OECD, 2017) in its bilateral tax treaties.

Recent developments

180. There are no recent developments with respect to element C.6.

Practical application

181. Up to date, the Isle of Man has incorporated an arbitration clause in six of its 24 treaties as a final stage to the MAP. In all six treaties its arbitration clause is equivalent to Article 25(5) of the OECD Model Tax Convention (OECD, 2017).

Anticipated modifications

182. The Isle of Man did not indicate that it anticipates any modifications in relation to element C.6.

Conclusion

	Areas for improvement	Recommendations
[C.6]	-	-

Notes

1. Available at: www.oecd.org/tax/dispute/mutual-agreement-procedure-statistics.htm. These statistics are up to and include fiscal year 2017.

2. For post-2015 cases, if the number of MAP cases in the Isle of Man's inventory at the beginning of the Statistics Reporting Period plus the number of MAP cases started during the Statistics Reporting Period was more than five, the Isle of Man reports its MAP caseload on a jurisdiction-by-jurisdiction basis. This rule applies for each type of cases (attribution/allocation cases and other cases).

3. The Isle of Man's 2018 MAP statistics were corrected in the course of its peer review and deviate from the published MAP statistics for 2018. See further details in Annex C.

References

OECD (2015), "Making Dispute Resolution Mechanisms More Effective, Action 14 – 2015 Final Report", in *OECD/G20 Base Erosion and Profit Shifting Project*, OECD Publishing, Paris, https://dx.doi.org/10.1787/9789264241633-en.

OECD (2017), *Model Tax Convention on Income and on Capital 2017 (Full Version)*, OECD Publishing, Paris, https://dx.doi.org/10.1787/g2g972ee-en.

Part D

Implementation of MAP agreements

[D.1] Implement all MAP agreements

> Jurisdictions should implement any agreement reached in MAP discussions, including by making appropriate adjustments to the tax assessed in transfer pricing cases.

183.   In order to provide full certainty to taxpayers and the jurisdictions, it is essential that all MAP agreements are implemented by the competent authorities concerned.

Legal framework to implement MAP agreements

184.   The Isle of Man reported that it has a domestic statute of limitation for both upward and downward adjustments.

185.   Concerning upward adjustments, sections 84A and 107 of the Income Tax Act 1970 define this statute of limitation as:

- six years after the end of the year of assessment to which it relates (for individuals)
- four years after the end of the accounting period (for companies).

186.   Concerning downward adjustments, section 55(1) of the Income Tax Act Income Tax define the statute of limitations as six years for individuals and four years for companies. In both cases, the starting point is the time when such assessments or adjustments have been made, either by the Isle of Man or by its treaty partner.

187.   The Isle of Man clarified that Section 104E(1) of the Income Tax Act 1970 stipulates that an international arrangement has effect despite any enactment or other document or any other rule of law. In relation to MAP agreements, it explained that this section would support the implementation of a resolution made under the MAP process by way of an assessment raised under domestic law. Consequently, the domestic statute of limitation in the Isle of Man does not prevent the implementation of any MAP agreements.

188.   With respect to the process for implementing MAP agreements, the Isle of Man reported that there are no specific rules in place nor is the taxpayer asked approval of the agreement reached. Where the MAP request entails a relief of double taxation to be provided by the Isle of Man, such relief can be provided by a deduction against the Isle of Man's income or via a tax credit.

Recent developments

189.   There are no recent developments with respect to element D.1.

Practical application

Period 1 January 2016-31 March 2019 (stage 1)

190.   The Isle of Man reported that in the period 1 January 2016-31 March 2019 it did not enter into any MAP agreement.

191.   Peers did not provide input in relation to the Isle of Man's implementation of the Action 14 Minimum Standard.

Period 1 April 2019-31 December 2020 (stage 2)

192.   The Isle of Man reported that since 1 April 2019 its competent authority has entered into one MAP agreement. This agreement, however, did not require implementation by the Isle of Man.

193.   The peer that provided input during stage 2 did not provide input in relation to element D.1.

Anticipated modifications

194.   The Isle of Man did not indicate that it anticipates any modifications in relation to element D.1.

Conclusion

	Areas for improvement	Recommendations
[D.1]	-	-

[D.2]   Implement all MAP agreements on a timely basis

> Agreements reached by competent authorities through the MAP process should be implemented on a timely basis.

195.   Delay of implementation of MAP agreements may lead to adverse financial consequences for both taxpayers and competent authorities. To avoid this and to increase certainty for all parties involved, it is important that the implementation of any MAP agreement is not obstructed by procedural and/or statutory delays in the jurisdictions concerned.

Theoretical timeframe for implementing mutual agreements

196.   The Isle of Man reported that its competent authority will ensure that MAP agreements are implemented on a timely basis including by making appropriate adjustments to the tax assessed, e.g. in transfer pricing cases. The Isle of Man added that once a MAP agreement has been implemented and the taxpayer's income tax assessment is revised, any refund will automatically be issued usually within two weeks of the date of the issue of the revised assessment.

Recent developments

197.   There are no recent developments with respect to element D.2.

Practical application

Period 1 January 2016-31 March 2019 (stage 1)

198. The Isle of Man reported that in the period 1 January 2016-31 March 2019, it did not enter into any MAP agreement.

199. Peers did not provide input in relation to the Isle of Man's implementation of the Action 14 Minimum Standard.

Period 1 April 2019-31 December 2020 (stage 2)

200. As described under element D.1, since 1 April 2019 the Isle of Man has entered into one MAP agreement, which did not require implementation in the Isle of Man.

201. The peer that provided input during stage 2 did not provide input in relation to element D.2.

Anticipated modifications

202. The Isle of Man did not indicate that it anticipates any modifications in relation to element D.2.

Conclusion

	Areas for improvement	Recommendations
[D.2]	-	-

[D.3] Include Article 25(2), second sentence, of the OECD Model Tax Convention in tax treaties or alternative provisions in Article 9(1) and Article 7(2)

> Jurisdictions should either (i) provide in their tax treaties that any mutual agreement reached through MAP shall be implemented notwithstanding any time limits in their domestic law, or (ii) be willing to accept alternative treaty provisions that limit the time during which a Contracting Party may make an adjustment pursuant to Article 9(1) or Article 7(2), in order to avoid late adjustments with respect to which MAP relief will not be available.

203. In order to provide full certainty to taxpayers it is essential that implementation of MAP agreements is not obstructed by any time limits in the domestic law of the jurisdictions concerned. Such certainty can be provided by either including the equivalent of Article 25(2), second sentence, of the OECD Model Tax Convention (OECD, 2017) in tax treaties, or alternatively, setting a time limit in Article 9(1) and Article 7(2) for making adjustments to avoid that late adjustments obstruct granting of MAP relief.

Legal framework and current situation of the Isle of Man's tax treaties

204. As discussed under element D.1, the Isle of Man's domestic legislation includes a statute of limitations of four to six years, but this would not be applicable as regards the implementation of MAP agreements.

205.   Out of the Isle of Man's 24 tax treaties, 22 contain a provision equivalent to Article 25(2), second sentence, of the OECD Model Tax Convention (OECD, 2017) that any mutual agreement reached through MAP shall be implemented notwithstanding any time limits in their domestic law. The remaining two neither contain such equivalent nor the alternative provisions for Article 9(1) and 7(2) setting a time limit for making transfer pricing adjustments.

206.   One peer provided input during stage 1 and mentioned that its treaty with the Isle of Man is a treaty with a limited scope that applies to a narrower range of circumstances than the MAP articles contained in comprehensive tax treaties. The peer further reported that it has not sought to amend its MAP article in order to meet the requirements under the Action 14 minimum standard. It also did not indicate it was contacted by the Isle of Man for this purpose.

Recent developments

Bilateral modifications

207.   There are no recent developments as to new treaties or amendments to existing treaties being signed in relation to element D.3.

Multilateral Instrument

208.   The Isle of Man signed the Multilateral Instrument and deposited its instrument of ratification on 25 October 2017. The Multilateral Instrument for the Isle of Man entered into force on 1 July 2018.

209.   Article 16(4)(b)(ii) of that instrument stipulates that Article 16(2), second sentence – containing the equivalent of Article 25(2), second sentence, of the OECD Model Tax Convention (OECD, 2017) – will apply in the absence of a provision in tax treaties that is equivalent to Article 25(2), second sentence, of the OECD Model Tax Convention (OECD, 2017). In other words, in the absence of this equivalent, Article 16(4)(b)(ii) of the Multilateral Instrument will modify the applicable tax treaty to include such equivalent. However, this shall only apply if both contracting parties to the applicable tax treaty have listed this treaty as a covered tax agreement under the Multilateral Instrument and insofar as both, pursuant to Article 16(6)(c)(ii), notified the depositary that this treaty does not contain the equivalent of Article 25(2), second sentence, of the OECD Model Tax Convention (OECD, 2017). Article 16(4)(b)(ii) of the Multilateral Instrument will for a tax treaty not take effect if one or both of the treaty partners has, pursuant to Article 16(5)(c), reserved the right not to apply the second sentence of Article 16(2) of that instrument for all of its covered tax agreements under the condition that: (i) any MAP agreement shall be implemented notwithstanding any time limits in the domestic laws of the contracting states, or (ii) the jurisdiction intends to meet the Action 14 Minimum Standard by accepting in its tax treaties the alternative provisions to Article 9(1) and 7(2) concerning the introduction of a time limit for making transfer pricing profit adjustments.

210.   In regard of the two tax treaties identified above that are considered not to contain the equivalent of Article 25(2), second sentence, of the OECD Model Tax Convention (OECD, 2017) or the alternative provisions for Articles 9(1) and 7(2), the Isle of Man listed none of them as covered tax agreements under the Multilateral Instrument. Therefore, at this stage, none of the two tax treaties will be modified by the Multilateral Instrument to include the equivalent of Article 25(2), second sentence, of the OECD Model Tax Convention (OECD, 2017).

Peer input

211. The peer that provided input during stage 2 did not provide input in relation to their tax treaty with the Isle of Man.

Anticipated modifications

212. The Isle of Man further reported that for the two tax treaties that do not contain the equivalent of Article 25(2), second sentence, of the OECD Model Tax Convention (OECD, 2017) or both alternatives provided for in Articles 9(1) and 7(2) and that will not be modified by the Multilateral Instrument, it is awaiting a response from the treaty partners to its request of the initiation of bilateral negotiations to amend the treaties to meet the requirements under the Action 14 Minimum Standard.

213. The Isle of Man reported it will seek to include Article 25(2), first sentence, of the OECD Model Tax Convention (OECD, 2017) in all of its future tax treaties.

Conclusion

	Areas for improvement	Recommendations
[D.3]	Two out of 24 tax treaties neither contain a provision that is equivalent to Article 25(2), second sentence, of the OECD Model Tax Convention (OECD, 2017) nor both alternative provisions provided for in Article 9(1) and Article 7(2). None of these treaties will be modified by the Multilateral Instrument to include the required provision. With respect to these two treaties, the Isle of Man has reached out to its treaty partners to request the initiation of bilateral negotiations, for which it is awaiting a response.	As the two treaties that do not contain the equivalent of Article 25(2), second sentence, of the OECD Model Tax Convention (OECD, 2017) will not be modified via the Multilateral Instrument, the Isle of Man should, upon receipt of a response from the relevant treaty partners agreeing to include the required provision or be willing to accept the inclusion of both alternative provisions, work towards updating the treaties to include this provision.

Reference

OECD (2017), *Model Tax Convention on Income and on Capital 2017 (Full Version)*, OECD Publishing, Paris, https://dx.doi.org/10.1787/g2g972ee-en.

Summary

	Areas for improvement	Recommendations
	Part A: Preventing disputes	
[A.1]	Two out of 23 tax treaties do not contain a provision that is equivalent to Article 25(3), first sentence, of the OECD Model Tax Convention (OECD, 2017). These two treaties will not be modified by the Multilateral Instrument to include the required provision, but the Isle of Man has reached out to its treaty partners to request the initiation of bilateral negotiations, for which it is awaiting a response.	For the two treaties that do not contain the equivalent of Article 25(3), first sentence, of the OECD Model Tax Convention (OECD, 2017) and that will not be modified by the Multilateral Instrument, the Isle of Man should, upon receipt of a response from the relevant treaty partners agreeing to include the required provision, work towards updating the treaties to include this provision
[A.2]	-	-
	Part B: Availability and access to MAP	
[B.1]	One out of 24 tax treaties does not contain a provision that is equivalent to Article 25(1), first sentence, of the OECD Model Tax Convention (OECD, 2017). This tax treaty will not be modified by the Multilateral Instrument to include the required provision. With respect to this treaty, negotiations are pending.	For the treaty that does not contain the equivalent of Article 25(1), first sentence, of the OECD Model Tax Convention (OECD, 2017) and will not be modified by the Multilateral Instrument to include such equivalent, the Isle of Man should continue negotiations to include the required provision. This concerns a provision that is equivalent to Article 25(1), first sentence, of the OECD Model Tax Convention (OECD, 2017) either: a. as amended by the Action 14 final report (OECD, 2015b); or b. as it read prior to the adoption of the Action 14 final report (OECD, 2015b), thereby including the full sentence of such provision.
	Two out of 24 tax treaties do not contain a provision that is equivalent to Article 25(1), first sentence, of the OECD Model Tax Convention (OECD, 2017) and the timeline to file a MAP request is three years, but only applies to transfer pricing adjustments. None of these two tax treaties will be modified by the Multilateral Instrument to include the first and second sentence of Article 25(1). With respect to these treaties, the Isle of Man has reached out to its treaty partners to request the initiation of bilateral negotiations, for which it is awaiting a response.	As the two treaties that do not contain the equivalent of Article 25(1), first and second sentence, of the OECD Model Tax Convention (OECD, 2017) will not be modified by the Multilateral Instrument to include such equivalent, the Isle of Man should, upon receipt of a response from the relevant treaty partners agreeing to include the required provision, work towards updating the treaties to include this provision.
[B.2]	-	-
[B.3]	-	-
[B.4]	-	-
[B.5]	-	-
[B.6]	-	-
[B.7]	-	-

	Areas for improvement	Recommendations
[B.8]	-	-
[B.9]	-	-
[B.10]	-	-
Part C: Resolution of MAP cases		
[C.1]	Three out of 24 tax treaties do not contain a provision that is equivalent to Article 25(2), first sentence, of the OECD Model Tax Convention (OECD, 2017). None of these treaties will be modified by the Multilateral Instrument to include the required provision. With respect to these three treaties,: • The Isle of Man has reached out to two treaty partners to request the initiation of bilateral negotiations, for which it is awaiting a response. • For one, negotiations were finalised.	For two of the three treaties that do not contain the equivalent of Article 25(2), first sentence, of the OECD Model Tax Convention (OECD, 2017) and will not be modified via the Multilateral Instrument, the Isle of Man should, upon receipt of a response from the relevant treaty partners agreeing to include the required provision, work towards updating the treaties to include this provision. Furthermore, for the third treaty, the Isle of Man should as quickly as possible sign and ratify the amending protocol to have in place the required provision.
[C.2]	-	-
[C.3]	-	-
[C.4]	-	-
[C.5]	-	-
[C.6]	-	-
Part D: Implementation of MAP agreements		
[D.1]	-	-
[D.2]	-	-
[D.3]	Two out of 24 tax treaties neither contain a provision that is equivalent to Article 25(2), second sentence, of the OECD Model Tax Convention (OECD, 2017) nor both alternative provisions provided for in Article 9(1) and Article 7(2). None of these treaties will be modified by the Multilateral Instrument to include the required provision. With respect to these two treaties, the Isle of Man has reached out to its treaty partners to request the initiation of bilateral negotiations, for which it is awaiting a response.	As the two treaties that do not contain the equivalent of Article 25(2), second sentence, of the OECD Model Tax Convention (OECD, 2017) will not be modified via the Multilateral Instrument, the Isle of Man should, upon receipt of a response from the relevant treaty partners agreeing to include the required provision or be willing to accept the inclusion of both alternative provisions, work towards updating the treaties to include this provision.

Annex A

Tax treaty network of the Isle of Man

Treaty partner	DTC in force?	Article 25(1) of the OECD Model Tax Convention ("MTC")		Article 9(2) of the OECD MTC	Anti-abuse	Article 25(2) of the OECD MTC		Article 25(3) of the OECD MTC		Arbitration
		B.1	B.1	B.3	B.4	C.1	D.3	A.1	B.7	. C.6
Column 1	Column 2	Column 3	Column 4	Column 5	Column 6	Column 7	Column 8	Column 9	Column 10	Column 11
		Inclusion Art. 25(1) first sentence? / If yes, submission to either competent authority? (new Art. 25(1), first sentence)	Inclusion Art. 25(1) second sentence? (Note 1)	Inclusion Art. 9(2) (Note 2) If no, will your CA provide access to MAP in TP cases?	Inclusion provision that MAP Article will not be available in cases where your jurisdiction is of the assessment that there is an abuse of the DTC or of the domestic tax law? If no, will your CA accept a taxpayer's request for MAP in relation to such cases?	Inclusion Art. 25(2) first sentence? (Note 3)	Inclusion Art. 25(2) second sentence? (Note 4) If no, alternative provision in Art. 7 & 9 OECD MTC? (Note 4)	Inclusion Art. 25(3) first sentence? (Note 5)	Inclusion Art. 25(3) second sentence? (Note 6)	Inclusion arbitration provision?
Y = yes / N = signed pending ratification	If N, date of signing	E = yes, either CAs / O = yes, only one CA / N = No	Y = yes / i = no, no such provision / ii = no, different period / iii = no, starting point for computing the 3 year period is different / iv = no, other reasons	Y = yes / i = no, but access will be given to TP cases / ii = no and access will not be given to TP cases	Y = yes / i = no and such cases will be accepted for MAP / ii = no but such cases will not be accepted for MAP	Y = yes / N = no	Y = yes / i = no, but have Art 7 equivalent / ii = no, but have Art 9 equivalent / iii = no, but have both Art. 7 & 9 equivalent / N = no and no equivalent of Art. 7 and 9	Y = yes / N = no	Y = yes / N = no	Y = yes / N = no
			If ii, specify period							
Australia	Y	N/A	N/A	N/A		N	N	N	N	N
		N	iv		i					
Bahrain	Y	N/A	N/A	Y		Y	Y	Y	Y	Y
		O*	Y		i					
Belgium	N	7/16/2009	N/A	Y		Y	Y	Y	Y*	Y
		E*	Y		i					

Treaty partner (Column 1)	DTC in force? (Column 2)		Inclusion Art. 25(1) first sentence? / If yes, submission to either competent authority? (Column 3, B.1)	Inclusion Art. 25(1) second sentence? (Note 1) (Column 4, B.1)	If no, please state reasons	Inclusion Art. 9(2) (Note 2) — If no, will your CA provide access to MAP in TP cases? (Column 5, B.3)	Anti-abuse — If no, will your CA accept a taxpayer's request for MAP in relation to such cases? (Column 6, B.4)	Inclusion Art. 25(2) first sentence? (Note 3) (Column 7, C.1)	Inclusion Art. 25(2) second sentence? (Note 4) / If no, alternative provision in Art. 7 & 9 OECD MTC? (Column 8, D.3)	Inclusion Art. 25(3) first sentence? (Note 5) (Column 9, A.1)	Inclusion Art. 25(3) second sentence? (Note 6) (Column 10, B.7)	Inclusion arbitration provision? (Column 11, C.6)
Denmark	Y	N/A	O	Y	N/A	Y	i	Y	Y	Y	N	N
Estonia	Y	N/A	E*	Y	N/A	Y	i	Y	Y	Y	Y	N
Faroe Islands	Y	N/A	O	Y	N/A	N/A	i	Y	Y	Y	Y	N
Finland	Y	N/A	E	Y	N/A	Y	i	Y	Y	Y	N	N
Greenland	Y	N/A	O	Y	N/A	Y	i	Y	Y	Y	Y	N
Guernsey	Y	N/A	E	Y	N/A	Y	i	Y	Y	Y	N	Y
Iceland	Y	N/A	O	Y	N/A	Y	i	Y	Y	Y	Y	N
Ireland	Y	N/A	O	Y	N/A	N/A	i	N	Y	Y	N	N
Jersey	Y	N/A	O	Y	N/A	Y	i	Y	Y	Y	N	Y
Luxembourg	Y	N/A	E*	Y	N/A	Y	i	Y	Y	Y	Y	Y
Malta	Y	N/A	E*	Y	N/A	Y	i	Y	Y	Y	Y	N
Netherlands	Y	N/A	O	Y	N/A	Y	i	Y	Y	N	N	N
New Zealand	Y	N/A	N	iv	N/A	N/A	i	N	N	N	N	N
Norway	Y	N/A	O	Y	N/A	Y	i	Y	Y	Y	N	N
Poland	Y	N/A	N	Y	N/A	N/A	i	Y	Y	Y	N	N
Qatar	Y	N/A	E*	Y*	2-years	i	i	Y	Y	Y	Y	N
Seychelles	Y	N/A	O*	Y	N/A	Y	i	Y	Y	Y	Y	N
Singapore	Y	N/A	O	Y	N/A	i	i	Y	Y	Y	Y	N
Slovenia	Y	N/A	O	Y	N/A	N/A	i	Y	Y	Y	Y	N
Sweden	Y	N/A	O	Y	N/A	Y	i	Y	Y	Y	N	N
United Kingdom	Y	N/A	E	Y	N/A	Y	i	Y	Y	Y	Y	Y

Legend

E* The provision contained in this treaty was already in line with the requirements under this element of the Action 14 Minimum Standard, but has been modified by the Multilateral Instrument to allow the filing of a MAP request in either contracting state.

E** The provision contained in this treaty was not in line with the requirements under this element of the Action 14 Minimum Standard, but the treaty has been modified by the Multilateral Instrument and is now in line with this standard.

O* The provision contained in this treaty is already in line with the requirements under this element of the Action 14 Minimum Standard, but will be modified by the Multilateral Instrument upon entry into force for this specific treaty and will then allow the filing of a MAP request in either contracting state.

O/E**** The provision contained in this treaty is already in line with the requirements under this element of the Action 14 Minimum Standard, but will be or has been superseded by the Multilateral Instrument only to the extent that existing treaty provisions are incompatible with the relevant provision of the Multilateral Instrument.

Y* The provision contained in this treaty was not in line with the requirements under this element of the Action 14 Minimum Standard, but the treaty has been modified by the Multilateral Instrument and is now in line with this element of the Action 14 Minimum Standard.

Y** The provision contained in this treaty already included an arbitration provision, which has been replaced by part VI of the Multilateral Instrument containing a mandatory and binding arbitration procedure.

Y** The provision contained in this treaty did not include an arbitration provision, but part VI of the Multilateral Instrument applies, following which a mandatory and binding arbitration procedure is included in this treaty

i*/ii*/iv*/N* The provision contained in this treaty is not in line with the requirements under this element of the Action 14 Minimum Standard, but the treaty will be modified by the Multilateral Instrument upon entry into force for this specific treaty and will then be in line with this element of the Action 14 Minimum Standard.

i/iv**/N**** The provision contained in this treaty is not in line with the requirements under this element of the Action 14 Minimum Standard, but the treaty will be superseded by the Multilateral Instrument upon entry into force for this specific treaty only to the extent that existing treaty provisions are incompatible with the relevant provision of the Multilateral Instrument.

i*/ii**** The provision contained in this treaty was not in line with the requirements under this element of the Action 14 Minimum Standard, but the treaty has been superseded by the Multilateral Instrument only to the extent that existing treaty provisions are incompatible with the relevant provision of the Multilateral Instrument.

Annex B

MAP statistics reporting for pre-2016 cases (1 January 2016 to 31 December 2020)

2016 MAP Statistics

Category of cases	No. of pre-2016 cases in MAP inventory on 1 January 2016	Number of pre-2016 cases closed during the reporting period by outcome											No. of pre-2016 cases remaining in on MAP inventory on 31 December 2016	Average time taken (in months) for closing pre-2016 cases during the reporting period
		Denied MAP access	Objection is not justified	Withdrawn by taxpayer	Unilateral relief granted	Resolved via domestic remedy	Agreement fully eliminating double taxation/ fully resolving taxation not in accordance with tax treaty	Agreement partially eliminating double taxation/partially resolving taxation not in accordance with tax treaty	Agreement that there is no taxation not in accordance with tax treaty	No agreement, including agreement to disagree	Any other outcome		
Column 1	Column 2	Column 3	Column 4	Column 5	Column 6	Column 7	Column 8	Column 9	Column 10	Column 11	Column 12	Column 13	Column 14
Attribution/ Allocation	0	0	0	0	0	0	0	0	0	0	0	0	N/A
Others	0	0	0	0	0	0	0	0	0	0	0	0	N/A
Total	0	0	0	0	0	0	0	0	0	0	0	0	N/A

2017 MAP Statistics

Category of cases	No. of pre-2016 cases in MAP inventory on 1 January 2017	Number of pre-2016 cases closed during the reporting period by outcome											No. of pre-2016 cases remaining in on MAP inventory on 31 December 2017	Average time taken (in months) for closing pre-2016 cases during the reporting period
		Denied MAP access	Objection is not justified	Withdrawn by taxpayer	Unilateral relief granted	Resolved via domestic remedy	Agreement fully eliminating double taxation/ fully resolving taxation not in accordance with tax treaty	Agreement partially eliminating double taxation/partially resolving taxation not in accordance with tax treaty	Agreement that there is no taxation not in accordance with tax treaty	No agreement, including agreement to disagree	Any other outcome		
Column 1	Column 2	Column 3	Column 4	Column 5	Column 6	Column 7	Column 8	Column 9	Column 10	Column 11	Column 12	Column 13	Column 14
Attribution/ Allocation	0	0	0	0	0	0	0	0	0	0	0	0	N/A
Others	0	0	0	0	0	0	0	0	0	0	0	0	N/A
Total	0	0	0	0	0	0	0	0	0	0	0	0	N/A

2018 MAP Statistics

Category of cases	No. of pre-2016 cases in MAP inventory on 1 January 2018	Number of pre-2016 cases closed during the reporting period by outcome										No. of pre-2016 cases remaining in on MAP inventory on 31 December 2018	Average time taken (in months) for closing pre-2016 cases during the reporting period
		Denied MAP access	Objection is not justified	Withdrawn by taxpayer	Unilateral relief granted	Resolved via domestic remedy	Agreement fully eliminating double taxation/fully resolving taxation not in accordance with tax treaty	Agreement partially eliminating double taxation/partially resolving taxation not in accordance with tax treaty	Agreement that there is no taxation not in accordance with tax treaty	No agreement, including agreement to disagree	Any other outcome		
Column 1	Column 2	Column 3	Column 4	Column 5	Column 6	Column 7	Column 8	Column 9	Column 10	Column 11	Column 12	Column 13	Column 14
Attribution/ Allocation	0	0	0	0	0	0	0	0	0	0	0	0	N/A
Others	0	0	0	0	0	0	0	0	0	0	0	0	N/A
Total	0	0	0	0	0	0	0	0	0	0	0	0	N/A

2019 MAP Statistics

Category of cases	No. of pre-2016 cases in MAP inventory on 1 January 2019	Number of pre-2016 cases closed during the reporting period by outcome										No. of pre-2016 cases remaining in on MAP inventory on 31 December 2019	Average time taken (in months) for closing pre-2016 cases during the reporting period
		Denied MAP access	Objection is not justified	Withdrawn by taxpayer	Unilateral relief granted	Resolved via domestic remedy	Agreement fully eliminating double taxation/fully resolving taxation not in accordance with tax treaty	Agreement partially eliminating double taxation/partially resolving taxation not in accordance with tax treaty	Agreement that there is no taxation not in accordance with tax treaty	No agreement, including agreement to disagree	Any other outcome		
Column 1	Column 2	Column 3	Column 4	Column 5	Column 6	Column 7	Column 8	Column 9	Column 10	Column 11	Column 12	Column 13	Column 14
Attribution/ Allocation	0	0	0	0	0	0	0	0	0	0	0	0	N/A
Others	0	0	0	0	0	0	0	0	0	0	0	0	N/A
Total	0	0	0	0	0	0	0	0	0	0	0	0	N/A

2020 MAP Statistics

Category of cases	No. of pre-2016 cases in MAP inventory on 1 January 2020	Number of pre-2016 cases closed during the reporting period by outcome											No. of pre-2016 cases remaining in on MAP inventory on 31 December 2020	Average time taken (in months) for closing pre-2016 cases during the reporting period
		Denied MAP access	Objection is not justified	Withdrawn by taxpayer	Unilateral relief granted	Resolved via domestic remedy	Agreement fully eliminating double taxation/ fully resolving taxation not in accordance with tax treaty	Agreement partially eliminating double taxation/partially resolving taxation not in accordance with tax treaty	Agreement that there is no taxation not in accordance with tax treaty	No agreement, including agreement to disagree	Any other outcome		
Column 1	Column 2	Column 3	Column 4	Column 5	Column 6	Column 7	Column 8	Column 9	Column 10	Column 11	Column 12	Column 13	Column 14
Attribution/ Allocation	0	0	0	0	0	0	0	0	0	0	0	0	N/A
Others	0	0	0	0	0	0	0	0	0	0	0	0	N/A
Total	0	0	0	0	0	0	0	0	0	0	0	0	N/A

Annex C

MAP statistics reporting for post-2015 cases (1 January 2016 to 31 December 2020)

2016 MAP Statistics

Category of cases	No. of post-2015 cases in MAP inventory on 1 January 2016	No. of post-2015 cases started during the reporting period	Denied MAP access	Objection is not justified	Withdrawn by taxpayer	Unilateral relief granted	Resolved via domestic remedy	Agreement fully eliminating double taxation/ fully resolving taxation not in accordance with tax treaty	Agreement partially eliminating double taxation/partially resolving taxation not in accordance with tax treaty	Agreement that there is no taxation not in accordance with tax treaty	No agreement, including agreement to disagree	Any other outcome	No. of post-2015 cases remaining in on MAP inventory on 31 December 2016	Average time taken (in months) for closing post-2015 cases during the reporting period
								Number of post-2015 cases closed during the reporting period by outcome						
Column 1	Column 2	Column 3	Column 4	Column 5	Column 6	Column 7	Column 8	Column 9	Column 10	Column 11	Column 12	Column 13	Column 14	Column 15
Attribution/ Allocation	0	0	0	0	0	0	0	0	0	0	0	0	0	N/A
Others	0	0	0	0	0	0	0	0	0	0	0	0	0	N/A
Total	0	0	0	N/A	0	0	0	0	0	0	0	0	0	N/A

2017 MAP Statistics

Category of cases	No. of post-2015 cases in MAP inventory on 1 January 2017	No. of post-2015 cases started during the reporting period	Denied MAP access	Objection is not justified	Withdrawn by taxpayer	Unilateral relief granted	Resolved via domestic remedy	Agreement fully eliminating double taxation/ fully resolving taxation not in accordance with tax treaty	Agreement partially eliminating double taxation/partially resolving taxation not in accordance with tax treaty	Agreement that there is no taxation not in accordance with tax treaty	No agreement, including agreement to disagree	Any other outcome	No. of post-2015 cases remaining in on MAP inventory on 31 December 2017	Average time taken (in months) for closing post-2015 cases during the reporting period
								Number of post-2015 cases closed during the reporting period by outcome						
Column 1	Column 2	Column 3	Column 4	Column 5	Column 6	Column 7	Column 8	Column 9	Column 10	Column 11	Column 12	Column 13	Column 14	Column 15
Attribution/ Allocation	0	0	0	0	0	0	0	0	0	0	0	0	0	N/A
Others	0	0	0	0	0	0	0	0	0	0	0	0	0	N/A
Total	0	0	0	0	0	0	0	0	0	0	0	0	0	N/A

2018 MAP Statistics

Category of cases	No. of post-2015 cases in MAP inventory on 1 January 2018	No. of post-2015 cases started during the reporting period	Number of post-2015 cases closed during the reporting period by outcome											No. of post-2015 cases remaining in on MAP inventory on 31 December 2018	Average time taken (in months) for closing post-2015 cases during the reporting period
			Denied MAP access	Objection is not justified	Withdrawn by taxpayer	Unilateral relief granted	Resolved via domestic remedy	Agreement fully eliminating double taxation/ fully resolving taxation not in accordance with tax treaty	Agreement partially eliminating double taxation/partially resolving taxation not in accordance with tax treaty	Agreement that there is no taxation not in accordance with tax treaty	No agreement, including agreement to disagree	Any other outcome		
Column 1	Column 2	Column 3	Column 4	Column 5	Column 6	Column 7	Column 8	Column 9	Column 10	Column 11	Column 12	Column 13	Column 14	Column 15
Attribution/ Allocation	0	0	0	0	0	0	0	0	0	0	0	0	0	N/A
Others	0	1	0	0	0	0	0	0	0	0	0	0	1	N/A
Total	0	1	0	0	0	0	0	0	0	0	0	0	1	N/A

2019 MAP Statistics

Category of cases	No. of post-2015 cases in MAP inventory on 1 January 2019	No. of post-2015 cases started during the reporting period	Number of post-2015 cases closed during the reporting period by outcome											No. of post-2015 cases remaining in on MAP inventory on 31 December 2019	Average time taken (in months) for closing post-2015 cases during the reporting period
			Denied MAP access	Objection is not justified	Withdrawn by taxpayer	Unilateral relief granted	Resolved via domestic remedy	Agreement fully eliminating double taxation/ fully resolving taxation not in accordance with tax treaty	Agreement partially eliminating double taxation/partially resolving taxation not in accordance with tax treaty	Agreement that there is no taxation not in accordance with tax treaty	No agreement, including agreement to disagree	Any other outcome		
Column 1	Column 2	Column 3	Column 4	Column 5	Column 6	Column 7	Column 8	Column 9	Column 10	Column 11	Column 12	Column 13	Column 14	Column 15
Attribution/ Allocation	0	0	0	0	0	0	0	0	0	0	0	0	0	N/A
Others	1	0	0	0	0	0	0	1	0	0	0	0	0	13.55
Total	1	0	0	0	0	0	0	1	0	0	0	0	0	13.55

2020 MAP Statistics

Category of cases	No. of post-2015 cases in MAP inventory on 1 January 2020	No. of post-2015 cases started during the reporting period	Number of post-2015 cases closed during the reporting period by outcome											No. of post-2015 cases remaining in on MAP inventory on 31 December 2020	Average time taken (in months) for closing post-2015 cases during the reporting period
			Denied MAP access	Objection is not justified	Withdrawn by taxpayer	Unilateral relief granted	Resolved via domestic remedy	Agreement fully eliminating double taxation/ fully resolving taxation not in accordance with tax treaty	Agreement partially eliminating double taxation/partially resolving taxation not in accordance with tax treaty	Agreement that there is no taxation not in accordance with tax treaty	No agreement, including agreement to disagree	Any other outcome		
Column 1	Column 2	Column 3	Column 4	Column 5	Column 6	Column 7	Column 8	Column 9	Column 10	Column 11	Column 12	Column 13	Column 14	Column 15
Attribution/ Allocation	0	0	0	0	0	0	0	0	0	0	0	0	0	N/A
Others	0	0	0	0	0	0	0	0	0	0	0	0	0	N/A
Total	0	0	0	0	0	0	0	0	0	0	0	0	0	N/A

Glossary

Action 14 Minimum Standard	The minimum standard as agreed upon in the final report on Action 14: Making Dispute Resolution Mechanisms More Effective
MAP guidance	Guidance Note 57 – Mutual Agreement Procedure in the Isle of Man's Double Taxation Agreements
MAP Statistics Reporting Framework	Rules for reporting of MAP statistics as agreed by the FTA MAP Forum
Multilateral Instrument	Multilateral Convention to Implement Tax Treaty Related Measures to Prevent Base Erosion and Profit Shifting
OECD Model Tax Convention	OECD Model Tax Convention on Income and on Capital as it read on 21 November 2017
OECD Transfer Pricing Guidelines	OECD Transfer Pricing Guidelines for Multinational Enterprises and Tax Administrations
Pre-2016 cases	MAP cases in a competent authority's inventory that are pending resolution on 31 December 2015
Post-2015 cases	MAP cases that are received by a competent authority from the taxpayer on or after 1 January 2016
Statistics Reporting Period	Period for reporting MAP statistics that started on 1 January 2016 and that ended on 31 December 2020
Terms of Reference	Terms of reference to monitor and review the implementing of the BEPS Action 14 Minimum Standard to make dispute resolution mechanisms more effective

Printed in Great Britain
by Amazon

23662632R00044